PARANORMAL
EASTBOURNE

JANET CAMERON

AMBERLEY

ACKNOWLEDGEMENTS

Many thanks to all the following, who have offered such friendly assistance and support in the writing of this book:

Mick Bony and the members of the gbhw team, Christopher Cope, Stuart and Jo Crook, Geraldine Curren, Richard Gardner, Mike Hawkins, Leah Hughes, Peter and Alex Killik, Margaret Mander, Tristan Morell, Danny Penman, Jonathan Poole, Charlie Prangnell, Martin Riddington, David Scanlan, K. J. Tagliaferro, Julie Van-Dungey.

Landlords, managers, bar staff and customers of all the wonderful, spooky pubs visited. (Chapter 6)

The staff at Local Studies, Eastbourne and The History Centre, Brighton, Seaford Library, Hove Library, the shop and café owners of Eastbourne Pier and the staff at Eastbourne Redoubt.

My editor Sarah Flight.

Unless otherwise indicated, all images are copyright of Janet Cameron.

First published 2010

Amberley Publishing
Cirencester Road, Chalford,
Stroud, Gloucestershire, GL6 8PE

www.amberleybooks.com

Copyright © Janet Cameron, 2010

The right of Janet Cameron to be identified as the Author of this work has been asserted in accordance with the Copyrights, Designs and Patents Act 1988.

ISBN 978 1 84868 996 1

British Library Cataloguing in Publication Data.
A catalogue record for this book is available from the British Library.

Typesetting and Origination by Amberley Publishing.
Printed in Great Britain.

CONTENTS

Waves breaking on Eastbourne beach in 1910

Spooky Eastbourne today

INTRODUCTION

A ghost is: 'the soul of a dead person which supposedly manifests itself to the living visibly (as in a shadowy apparition), audibly, etc. This is the definition according to the Oxford Reference Dictionary. But can it really be as simple as that? Not if some of the following accounts are anything to go by. The paranormal, it seems, manifests in many fascinating and unexpected ways and Eastbourne, an elegant and historical seaside resort on England's south coast, is no stranger to its mysteries.

Early cultures believed in communication with the 'other side' – and their unshakeable faith continues to this day. The belief that exorcism can banish demons from those who are mentally disturbed or ill – or even just a little different from everyone else – is still central to many cultures. Faith in the paranormal doesn't just stop with phantom people either. We have 'ghost animals', 'ghost ships' and 'phantom trains', etc. Sometimes, whole armies are claimed to manifest themselves to those who are sensitive to spiritual phenomena, for example, the spectral army (or armies) claimed to appear outside the walls of Pevensey Castle.

The Emergence of Spiritualism

During the early nineteenth century, with the onset of spiritism, the belief that certain people could communicate with the dead became even more widely accepted. Today many people find comfort in believing that their departed loved ones are still close to them, maybe as angels, a belief resulting in the current popularity of psychics, mediums and clairvoyants.

Definitions of Words for Paranormal Activity

It's often suggested by paranormal investigators that a ghost is actually a memory, in other words, the residual energy in a location of a person who once lived or died there, in other words, a recording. A ghost is merely an apparition and cannot be aware of us – ghosts are simply not in our dimension and that is why they can glide through walls and float up and down staircases no longer there. For example, Pevensey's spectral armies are ghosts, not spirits.

A spirit, on the other hand, is a person who lived on earth and who has thrown off their physical body to pass beyond. But, for some reason – maybe unfinished business, trauma, a need for revenge or an inability to accept that they are actually dead – their spirit-in-limbo has returned to visit us here on earth. Now we are talking about a live intelligence. That's why a spirit can communicate with us, unlike a ghost. Luckily, most paranormal phenomena are benign and not the least interested in harming us, but just occasionally, you do get a phantom with real *issues*.

The word poltergeist means, literally, 'a noisy spirit'. Poltergeists can be mischievous and are said to be especially attracted to the energy of children and young adults. Or, maybe the poltergeist is actually generated by the energy of the child or young person. We cannot know for sure how poltergeists come to exist. What we do know is that they move things, hide things, switch equipment on and off, cause tapping and banging, start fires, slam doors and generally cause confusion and chaos. Sometimes they may be the spirits of former occupants of a house, who are unaware that they are dead and want to frighten the 'new' incumbents into leaving 'their' domain. But this doesn't always work. Sometimes the poltergeist follows its target to their new home – for whatever reason that is meaningful to a poltergeist!

Theories and Interpretations

Even so, while claims of human contact with the paranormal are universal and although they began in the ancient past, we should bear in mind that culture plays a part and that our interpretations of what we experience are dependent upon our own personal beliefs and the time and place in which we exist. What is for certain is that nothing is ever destroyed in our Universe; it simply changes into something else. It's that 'something else' that is the focus for this book. I have tried, as far as possible, to discover the human stories behind the phenomena, as well as their historical background, and sometimes have included more than one theory to explain a sighting or weird experience.

It should be borne in mind that some of these stories come from legends and old stories that have passed into local folklore, are widely recorded and discussed and often have a complex historical context. Where possible I have tried to follow these stories up and to update them with any modern-day experiences and sightings. Some stories are modern-day personal accounts from Eastbourne people that are sincerely believed and have been recorded as accurately as possible. It's up to you to make of them what you will, but to reserve judgement and continue to believe in what is right for you.

And again, some accounts defy any explanation. Whatever your personal convictions, I hope you will enjoy the stories, both old and new, and I would like to express my thanks to everyone who helped me to complete this book by sharing their ideas about the paranormal as well as their own spooky encounters.

I have taken care to acknowledge everyone who has helped me, either verbally or by email. I have included every publication I have used as background in my text and/or bibliography, but without citing every individual author where there have been multiple and/or similar accounts of paranormal activity. I have obtained copyright permission for all images used unless stated to be in the public domain. If I have unwittingly made any errors or omissions, please contact my publishers so this can be put right in future reprints. I have used either the first name or both names of people I have interviewed according to preference, but also respected requests for anonymity.

NB: As it's sometimes difficult to ascertain whether a paranormal phenomenon is a ghost or a spirit, I shall use 'ghost' or 'phantom' as my default position.

CHAPTER 1

THE GHOSTS THAT HAUNT EASTBOURNE PIER

Eastbourne Pier is absolutely *teeming* with ghosts. It may even be the UK's most haunted pier. The account of the soldier who haunts the outside of the nightclub is a famous story – for the others, I am indebted to Charlie Prangnell, who not only works at the pier in a number of capacities, but is also highly-sensitive to paranormal activity. Charlie's sightings date back to the early 1980s.

The Black Phantom in the Channel Bar

The year was 1983 and at this time most staff and workmen were scared of walking upstairs into what was to be the Channel Bar. All of them had sensed something not quite right about the place. Then, just before Christmas, the regular nightwatchman fell sick and Charlie had to take over his duties. When he was asked to do a nightwatch, he decided to set himself up to work all night on the renovation of the Channel Bar. He was the only living person on the pier and around 4.00 am, he was busy sawing some wood when a tall, black shape came towards him. It was wearing a black cape and a trilby-type black hat. Charlie was startled and tried to tell himself it was all in the mind, but insists, 'I know what I saw.'

A few minutes after the sighting, a big bauble from the Christmas decorations on the ceiling dropped down and bounced onto the top of Charlie's steps. Then it bounced, elegantly downwards, a step at a time – almost deliberately, instead of rolling as you would expect. 'Things like this always happen after 4.00 am,' says Charlie. 'It's obvious the ghost doesn't like us making all that noise during the night-time.'

Into the Void

Around the mid to late eighties, the area known as 'The Void' used to be an old balcony. This area suffered as the result of the pier's fire in 1970, but its steps remained intact. One day, Charlie was working in The Void, making tables for a trade fair. Throughout the night he was cutting wood with a jigsaw and he put down the jigsaw so he could turn over the wood. But when he went to use it again, it had stopped working.

Above: Eastbourne Pier, the pride and joy of the local people

Left: The Fortune Teller's board on Eastbourne Pier

Above: Eastbourne Pier, looking towards the seafront

Left: Lads' day out on Eastbourne Pier 1959, around the time that Charlie Prangnell was a lad himself. Copyright Janet Cameron

Charlie Prangnell is highly-sensitive to spirit vibrations

The black phantom walked from the far wall of this area towards Charlie. It's now being revamped as a function room.

The workroom in The Void where
Charlie's jigsaw shut itself off.

Confused, Charlie looked down to check the plug socket. It had been turned off – and
certainly not by Charlie.

Annoyed, Charlie told the interfering entity to go away. Fortunately, it did.

Swishing Batons

In the mid-eighties, around midsummer, a raft race around the pier was being organised.
Charlie's job was to make Indian canoes, so he set to work one night, using thin bits
of plywood, just about one inch wide. He'd dumped the plywood in a large dustbin
full of water; this was to make the material bendable for fashioning into the curved
shape required for canoes. He looked towards the six-foot long bin which was next
to a stand-lamp, and from the reflection in the water, Charlie saw that the plywood
batons were standing on end and swishing to and fro, entirely under their own volition.
Although the batons were clacking madly together, there was no noise. Charlie used
his 'magic word' (unprintable) to make it stop and it did.

The producers of a children's TV programme at that time, called *Mystery and
Imagination*, were intrigued by Charlie's experience and they came to Eastbourne to
film a re-enactment of the batons swishing to and fro.

The Balloon Factory

- At the end of the arcade stood the Royal Sovereign, a pub shaped like a ship, which was renamed The Balloon Factory. The nightwatchman always had the clocking-in key. The clocking-in took place on a wall behind the adjoining pub doors, where bingo was played. Two unconnected nightwatchmen independently reported hearing a banging sound and doors opening. Pots and pans and plates would suddenly start flying through the air and the men would have to duck and dodge them. Finally, it all became too much and Charlie's men refused to work or clean in the pub.
- In 1983, the air conditioning motor switched itself on and off from the mains.
- The Atlantis was formerly known as the Pavilion Showbar, and subsequently became the Roxy and the Oddysey before acquiring its present name, the Atlantis. A week after the balloon-popping incident above, Charlie was working upstairs one Thursday night in the Atlantis's Copa Club (the former Channel Bar). The staff didn't like going upstairs at night and Charlie was in a teasing mood. Wanting to wind them up, he said: 'Don't make a noise otherwise you'll wake up the ghost.' There were some balloons lying on the pool table and some mischievous girls went over and popped them. Getting into the spooky spirit of things, Charlie murmured: 'Is anybody there?' And suddenly there was a bright shiny flash. Someone said that one of the neon lights was flashing on and off. The weird thing was that the light wasn't even plugged in. Everyone was scared and left, except for Charlie who stayed to finish his work.
- Sometimes, at night, staff would hold a barbecue on the beach. One night the rain was pelting down, so they decided to have the barbecue in the Channel (Copa) Bar. The Waterfront café was sealed off, with all doors locked, so no one could get down into the area. Yet at 4.00 am all the alarms sounded. Charlie rushed to the call point to check. The 'break glass' alarm was intact. 'That's how I knew the ghost didn't like noise at night after 4.00 am,' says Charlie.
- Night security began at around 11.00 pm. One evening, Charlie was doing the security shift in his office next to the nightclub when there was an enormous crash, so he rushed to investigate. Every single stool, lining the bar shelving, had crashed to the floor, yet there was no one on the pier but Charlie.

  Later the pub became Burger King and the cellarman reported seeing an apparition walking through the place, although there have been no recent sightings recorded.

  The following stories of Eastbourne ghosts have not been among Charlie Prangnell's personal experiences, but sightings have been claimed by several independent eyewitnesses.

Eastbourne Pier's Bashful Ghost

If you decide, in spite of all the previous stories, to have a night out at the Eastbourne Pier's Atlantis Nightclub, you may decide to take a break for a breath of fresh, sea air outside. Don't be surprised if you see the phantom of a soldier in army uniform.

He won't be interested in you, though. This is a very timid ghost and as soon as he's spotted, he vanishes back through the wall.

The nightclub was once the site of the pier's theatre, the Starlight Theatre, but it burnt down in 1970. The soldier may have visited the beautiful Victorian pier for entertainment during the Second World War before returning to action and, possibly, sudden death.

This exquisite and well-maintained pier was originally built between 1866 and 1870, but then in 1877 it was broken clean in two by a storm. Where it was fixed, it was made to slope higher up, to prevent the stormy seas from destroying it again. It reopened in 1923.

Other Eastbourne Pier Ghosts:

- The ghost of a woman in black is said to join the dancers on the Atlantis dance floor. No one knows who she is, but Charlie Prangnell explains that during one season around the turn of the eighties into the nineties a horrible thing happened: six people actually died there; literally dropping down dead on the dance floor.
- A little boy ghost can occasionally be sighted in the cellar, sitting forlornly on a barrel.

CHAPTER 2

SOME PERSONAL STORIES OF HAUNTED EASTBOURNE

Throughout time, we have endeavoured to understand and explain the mysterious apparitions and fleeting images that impact so strangely on our lives. It is a fallacy that only castles and ancient buildings are haunted. You are just as likely to find a ghost in a suburban house or a modern shop or supermarket as in an ancient burial ground, old manor house or twelfth century castle. These are new, personal stories from Eastbourne people experienced in ordinary locations around the town.

The Haunted Boat at Eastbourne Marina

Mr. Peter Killik has lived in Eastbourne for over thirteen years and now runs the popular venue The Brazz in The Enterprise Centre, the subject of a separate story under

The Haunted Boat, with permission Mr. Peter Killick

Chapter 6, 'Ghosts in Pubs, Inns and Bars'. Peter tells a fascinating story about a ghost that haunted a restaurant boat, of which he was general manager with his partner in Eastbourne Marina, (see image). This was a mobile ghost, and it haunted every single space on the boat and often made tapping and knocking noises at night. Its favourite place was the engine room where it would mess around with the switches, turning them off and on. Peter says he could feel the intense chill as he walked past the engine room at night. In many ways, the paranormal activity resembled that of a poltergeist.

'I was always the last to leave the boat so I would search around and sometimes there were sudden bright flashes of lights that could not be explained,' says Peter.

The phone lines to the bridge would often be busy, even though no one was around, as though someone was trying, desperately, to contact the bridge. 'I was told there had once been a fatality on the boat,' explains Peter, 'but I don't know what happened or when it happened.'

The Weeping Child and the Phantom Family

Sara, who helps as a barmaid at The Brazz, told the story about a house in Meads Road alleged to be haunted by a little girl who often sat weeping on the stairs. The current occupiers were so freaked out by this pitiful apparition that they emigrated and moved to Canada. Some local people organised an exorcism in the house, but although they didn't witness the ghost of the little girl, something even stranger happened.

Apparently, a family had been killed in a car accident outside the house – and the exorcism revealed them trapped in a corner of the living room behind the television. It was clear someone had to help them. Fortunately, the exorcism was successful, and in time, the phantom family moved on to a higher level.

The Houseproud Ghost

Many people believe that spirits are around us all the time, watching us and even guiding us in our daily lives. Such a believer is clairvoyant and psychic, Tristan Morell, who once lived in a haunted house with his partner, Barry, in the Little Chelsea area in Eastbourne's town centre. The young men were haunted by the benign but feisty ghost of a little old lady. Tristan says she was happy when the young men moved in, but she didn't think much of their housekeeping skills.

Obsessive about cleanliness, she preferred everything tidy and was always busy turning taps on. 'Although she didn't do anything really useful, like the washing-up,' adds Tristan. But if the young men left their clothes lying around in a heap, she'd move them around, and once, when a friend stayed, her make-up was moved, as if the old lady ghost was trying to say, 'Put your things away properly in the cupboard'. She also hated extravagance and kept turning the heating down.

Tristan Morell, with permission T. Morell

Sadly, the couple eventually quarrelled and broke up. At that point, their old lady ghost went ballistic and started banging about upstairs, venting her anger.

Henry, the Caretaker Ghost

When clairvoyant and Reiki master, Julie Van-Dungey, moved into her house in Eastbourne in mid-June, 2009 with her partner, John, she found it already occupied – by 'Henry'. Julie wasn't surprised, as she'd already spotted her ghost looking down at her when she viewed the house outside in early May. Julie sensed Henry was lonely and that he was pleased that somebody would soon be moving in to keep him company. When she and John, her partner, walked around the house to the back garden, Henry moved into a back bedroom to continue to check out his new housemates.

Julie explains the house, which was an old guest-house, had not been occupied for about ten years. She continues, 'On occasion, Henry has brought guests home, invited by *him*. Although I'm not too sure how welcome they are by the humans that live here!' Mostly, she doesn't mind, except at night, when she is alone in the house and trying to sleep. 'I used to be so scared by night-time visitors; it's not a good feeling – having someone in the room whilst you are asleep.'

Julie has learned to handle those creepy feelings, and invites the unwanted guests to leave, explaining this is not a good time to be visiting. She says this usually works. (Although, on one occasion, she was frightened by a spirit that leant over her, and attempted to put an uncomfortable pressure on her chest.)

'This is not the first time I have lived with a ghost, or a spirit of the deceased,' explains Julie. 'In fact, we are surrounded every day, in all we do, by ghosts!' Julie, always sensitive to such things, was freaked out by such visits as a child – especially in the bathroom where you would expect to have your privacy! She says that some spirits are attached to a property while others cling to people. 'Henry feels attached to this property, almost as if he were a caretaker.'

Julie is convinced her resident ghost had never lived on the property in his physical form and adds that during the time she has lived in the house, his presence has gradually diminished. 'I think he is letting go as he knows the house is being taken care of. When the plaster was being removed in the basement, he was very unhappy and the whole house felt sad, but now that everything is re-plastered, the house just beams from the outside.'

Julie used her psychic skills to give Henry healing, asking the Angels to help him. As a result, when he does appear he is brighter and more enlightened. 'Freed, in a way, to move on,' says Julie. 'He is not around much now as I believe he has developed spiritually and can now move more freely between the different energy levels. Growth doesn't stop when we die; it's just easier to grow whilst we are in physical form – things that we see as trials and difficulties are opportunities for us to grow and develop spiritual qualities that will serve us when we physically 'die'.'

Julie says her partner John is a 'very down-to-earth builder' and does not experience the paranormal in any way – but he does believe her now about Henry.

To find out more about what Julie offers in the way of spiritual guidance, go to http://thewhitelightsanctuary.co.uk

Never Again!

When young Charlie Prangnell left home and got himself his own flat above a restaurant, he got in with a crowd of young people who wanted to hold a séance. 'Never again!' says the older and wiser Charlie.

'There was a glow from the red bulb in the electric fire, which made everything spookier. We started the séance and suddenly there was a sound of howling, just like a heavy wind, roaring through the house,' says Charlie. He adds that there was one unbeliever in the room – but by the end of the session he was too scared to go downstairs to the toilet on the lower floor.

One day, after a night out clubbing and enjoying himself, Charlie arrived at his flat at 3.00 am – to find his bed was wedged halfway down the stairs. It wasn't damaged so it hadn't been thrown. It was as though it had been lifted and placed there carefully by someone – or *something*. By now Charlie had had enough of shifting for himself. He speedily moved back to the comparative safety of the Royal Oak at Pevensey with his dad.

CHAPTER 3

OLD HAG SYNDROME

In cases of 'old hag syndrome' also known as 'sleep paralysis', a person wakes up but cannot move a muscle. They can see, hear, feel and smell but it's as though they are paralysed by a terrible pressure on their chest causing great difficulty in breathing. Accompanying this awful feeling, the victim also senses an overpowering, evil presence in the room.

The Wife who Came and Went

It's rare for a spirit to be hostile, but another event in Eastbourne occurred in the 1960s and was widely reported at the time. A family had moved into Watts Lane, and pretty soon, things started to happen. Furniture could be heard moving around, taps and switches turned themselves on and off, while doors opened and closed for no reason.

The worst thing of all happened one night when the man found he was unable to move his legs. To his horror, he actually saw a phantom pressing down on them. By now, the family was already feeling desperate and this final outrageous event was the last straw.

They took the logical next step and called in a priest to bless the house. The priest came to pray and to sprinkle holy water around. Fortunately the ceremony was successful, and the unwelcome guest was exorcised – or so it seemed. However, at that time, the man's wife had just moved out of the house, so it was difficult to know whether she was responsible for the ghost or whether the change was genuinely due to priestly intervention. But, sure enough, when the wife returned some years later, the paranormal activity resumed

On one occasion, the man witnessed someone walking up the stairs, when he knew there was no one there – at least, no one *human*. Again, there were voices, general noises, heavy furniture being shifted about and thudding across the floor. The family thought that it could have been the ghost of a previous owner, who had died some years before. Sometimes, previous incumbents who have failed to 'move on', view the new occupants as intruders, get angry and do whatever they can to get rid of them. On the other hand, considering the coincidence of the phenomena stopping and restarting in synchronicity with the wife's coming and going, that is a matter for conjecture. It certainly seems as though the ghost may have been a late owner of the cottages as the family suspected and that it had a hostile attitude to the wife of the new owner. But, by now the family had had more than enough and shortly after, they sold the house and moved away.

Martin's Sinister Encounter

Martin Riddington had just such an experience, and he insists he was not imagining it. It happened in the mid 1980s, when he stayed with friends in a large first-floor bedsit overlooking Pevensey Road, a short distance from where the British Legion was once located. Martin visited his friends for dinner and the three of them spent the evening relaxing and watching television. Then Martin fell asleep on the sofa and his friends covered him up with a blanket, then went to bed themselves.

During the night, Martin woke up, startled to hear a female voice calling his name. He glanced over to his right, in the direction of the sound. The only light in the room was from a nearby streetlight, which shone through the window behind the sofa. He says, 'It was enough for me to make out what I can only describe as a shapeless mist, combined with the shimmering you see on tarmac on a hot day. It kind of glided in front of the sofa, and said, 'Martin, I want you."

Martin struggled to get up into a sitting position, but found himself held back down by his wrists on either side of his head. He was unable to make a sound. After a short struggle, he thinks he lost consciousness. When he awoke in the morning, he told his shocked friends about his terrifying experience. 'I don't believe it was just a dream,' he says. He told his story to some of his other friends, and one of them reported a similar experience. In the friend's case, he didn't actually fall asleep, but the apparition gradually disappeared.

Martin's experience seems to bear a striking resemblance to incidents in two of the above-mentioned stories, the husband whose legs were held down in 'The Wife Who Came and Went' and, in the previous chapter under the subheading: 'Henry the Caretaker Ghost', where Julie felt a spirit pressing on her chest. Martin reports that some time later, he watched a television programme about the condition called 'sleep paralysis'. This led to an explanation of 'old hag syndrome' which is, allegedly, a common experience. A scientist on the programme explained that in his view, it wasn't a ghostly occurrence. But Martin is still unconvinced. 'Nobody's telling me I imagined it,' he says, but he has no idea who or what the female apparition was.

Early Beliefs about Old Hag Syndrome

The term 'old hag' originally referred to the superstition that a witch would land on and ride a person's chest. Another supernatural explanation was that an incubus, or a succubus was responsible, in other words, a fallen angel. Incubi appear to women, succubi to men. They may take the form of a fully grown person, or a satyr or a horrible, smelly old goat.

The Vampire by Philip Burne-Jones. Vampires are often blamed for experiences of Old Hag Syndrome

On the other hand, there may be a scientific explanation as suggested by scientists. One of a more pragmatic kind is that it could just be indigestion, but most people who experience the nightmare phenomenon seem to find that rather hard to accept.

CHAPTER 4

THE MAD, BAD LAUGHING ZOMBIE

Here is another instance of a place that is haunted, even though it is not old, or ruined or the location of some ghastly or traumatic event. According to a report by *Mail Online* (www.dailymail.co.uk) dated 15 February, 2008 employees of Southern Water's Sewage Treatment Works in Eastbourne were freaked out by a humanoid figure that appeared to stalk them in the works' underground tunnels. It had got to a point where the staff were far too scared to enter the tunnels, making it impossible for them to do their jobs properly. Mark Wey, one of the sewage treatment workers said that the zombie-like figure followed workers about, and even laughed at them. Sometimes muffled conversations could be heard behind the tunnel walls.

Jess Bauldry, in an article in *The Argus* dated 18 February 2008 said that hushed voices whispering in empty corridors, shadowy figures and orbs or balls of electromagnetic energy have all been heard or spotted at the waste-water treatment works in Prince William Parade in Eastbourne.

Mark Wey, who had worked at the treatment works for seven years, described how he saw a ghostly figure walk into a room out of the corner of his eye. On another occasion, the heavy doors to the control room swung open on their own. Another worker was convinced he was being watched when working in the chemical room. It became so frightening that Mark got permission from his bosses to call in a paranormal investigator and eventually Michael Kingscote, a parapsychologist, turned up at the works. He paid particular attention to one area where people claimed to have seen and felt things.

'Michael instantly detected someone standing there and he was suspicious there was something quite unusual there,' Mark Wey told the *Mail Online*. He added that it wasn't possible to prove a haunting. 'The conclusion is we can't prove it is haunted because of strong electromagnetic fields which can cause the illusion of being haunted, the feeling of being touched or watched, but there is definitely paranormal activity,' he says.

'People feel uneasy when they enter the building and the hairs on the back of your neck go up,' said Mark. 'A lot of people do not like going in there.'

Another member of staff commented: 'I believe in ghosts and I'm sure there's something there. I dread doing the night shift.' But the bosses were a little more cautious in their comments; as one spokesman said: 'Mr. Wey has a personal interest in the afterlife and found our underground site at Eastbourne somewhat spooky. We hope the findings weren't too frightening.'

However, according to *The Argus*, Mark and Michael Kingscote claimed to have photographic and audio evidence of the haunting. Mr. Kingscote is reported as saying: 'I'm prepared to say there's a higher than average amount of paranormal activity at the site. We have pictorial evidence that you can't dispute. You can clearly see facial features and shadowy figures.'

Yet most of the site was built in the eighties, while older parts only date back to 1969. Mr. Kingscote added that the plant has higher than average levels of electromagnetic energy because of the water and energy passing through it. Because of this, it acts as a magnet for paranormal activity from the surrounding area, rather than from the actual site. The clairvoyant also pointed out that he'd often got little response from investigating castles, normally believed to be prone to paranormal visitations. 'It's the council houses and modern living places where there's most activity,' he claimed.

Apparently there was a murder on the beach nearby in the twenties and one unfortunate person drowned on the site in one of the older parts. Reassuringly though, Mr. Kingscote felt that the drowned person was protective of the site's employees and that none of the presences were bad ones.

A word from the cynics: Ben Goldacre's article of 19 April 2008 about various psychic phenomena around the country, appeared on the website www.badscience. net. He quotes a plant worker at the Eastbourne site: 'It's not funny going to work and worrying that a zombie might be around the corner.' In response, Mr. Goldacre comments, 'It's even less funny for a consumer to be cynically exploited by a psychic, because everybody knows that, although psychics have their merits, they are entirely useless in this situation; to kill a zombie, you must destroy its brain.' A valid point, maybe.

The *Mail Online* report also attracted a response from no less than Richard Dawkins of Dallas, Texas who wrote the book *The God Delusion*. On 18 February, 2008 Mr. Dawkins wrote: 'This is a crazy idea, but could it be possible that there is a vagrant or a homeless person hiding in the tunnels? That seems more likely than a 'zombie' hiding down in a sewage plant. Instead of hiring a medium they should ask their bosses to have security carefully search the tunnels and make sure that a real person isn't actually living in their plant.' Of course, Richard Dawkins makes a fair point but it's still hard to imagine why even a homeless person would seek out shelter in a sewage plant of all places! But zombie, phantom or even 'strange homeless person with a liking for living somewhere smelly and underground', it must have been a truly terrifying experience for the plant workers.

CHAPTER 5

THE MUTINY AT THE BARRACKS AND THE GHOSTS LEFT BEHIND

When the troops were moved from their comfortable quarters near Portsmouth to the bleak Blatchington Barracks in 1795, they had a nasty shock coming. The Barracks were located between Seaford and Newhaven near to the coast, but it was to be a bitterly cold winter, and the Downs were covered with snow from January to as late as April 1795. There were sub-zero temperatures and there were banks of frost and ice that refused to melt.

The Seeds of Discontent

Of course, it's the trauma, pain and tragedy that usually create the ideal ambience for a haunting or hauntings. Certainly, in the case of the Blatchington mutineers, there was plenty of grief going on at the Barracks. In his book *The Seaford Mutiny of 1795*, Peter Longstaff-Tyrrell tells how the troops became distressed and angry, especially at the widely contrasting conditions between officers and troops. The men were cold, miserable and hungry. They were forced to make twelve mile marches to their training grounds – and all on virtually empty stomachs as the food rations were minimal and of poor quality.

On Thursday 16 April, some of the Oxford Militia reached breaking point. They targeted the premises of a butcher in Seaford. After breaking in, the men seized the juicy joints, and, elated in their triumph, they cavorted about town boasting of their exploits to anyone who would listen. The next day, they went even further. Five hundred men fixed their bayonets to march on the High Street at Seaford. They grabbed everything they could get their hands on, even selling off their goods to comrades at special prices.

Captain Thomas Harbon who belonged to the Seaford Volunteers, tried to persuade the mutineering men to surrender and some actually complied with this request. But the most stubborn rebels took off to Bishopstone Tide Mills where they purloined three hundred sacks of flour from a farm. Commandeering a sloop, the men caused it to go around Newhaven Bridge in order to deposit the booty in a warehouse, where sixty men remained on guard. The rest of the men returned to the Barracks.

The Trial

Certain men were charged as guilty of being the ringleaders of the uprising within the Regiment, and so it was decided they would have to pay the price. The trial took place on 5 May 1795 at Brighton's Old Ship Hotel. The outcome of the Trial would be grim. The official line was that there should be severe and instant reprisal for any insurrection. Clearly, a severe punishment would serve as a deterrent to others considering mutiny as an option – and so the supposed ringleaders were doomed.

The Execution

The execution took place on Saturday 13 June at Goldstone Bottom, a national ampitheatre in Hove. This area was the site of a horrible act in 1793 when the highwayman, James Rooke's tarred corpse was on view in an iron gibbet – for a year! James Rooke had killed a postal courier.

The two men, Edward Cooke from Witney and Henry Parish from Chipping Norton had been accused of instigating the mutiny. They arrived at 5.00am in good time for their execution at 8.30am and were forced to kneel down beside their coffins. Both died bravely and it's reported by Mr. Longstaff-Tyrrell that strong soldiers were reduced to tears by the cruel scene. Apparently, Edward Cooke himself gave the order to fire.

The Oxford Militia mutineers were to be buried in an unmarked grave near a perimeter wall at St. Andrews Church at Bishopstone. Two other men, James Sykes and William Sampson were also hanged that day,

The Consequence – Souls that Cannot Rest

It was claimed that the haunting of the Barracks must have been due to the angry, displaced spirits of the men sacrificed, allegedly as scapegoats, to pay for the crimes of the Regiment in general. The Highlanders, who were later quartered there, insisted they had seen the apparitions and, according to Peter Longstaff-Tyrrell's book, quoting from the *Sussex Weekly Advertiser* of 21 December 1795, some of the men had claimed they'd had 'conferences' with them. This seems to suggest they may have actually spoken with them, which implies that these were spirits rather than ghosts. The paper says: 'Reason and argument have been exerted to prove to them the fallacy of such superstition and absurd notions, but in no vain.'

Edward Cooke, who died in front of the firing squad that day, was subsequently known as 'Captain Cooke' because, it is said that he led the mutiny.

The Last Goodbye

At the end of 1795, the Oxfords were able to leave the dreaded Blatchington Barracks, which closed when the camp was demolished in 1818.

The Martello Towers

There were 103 conical Martello Towers erected between 1804 and 1810 and which ranged from East Anglia to Seaford. The Tower at Eastbourne, No. 65, fell into the sea in 1938.

<hr>

CHAPTER 6

GHOSTS IN PUBS, INNS AND BARS

Pubs, inns and bars provide fertile hunting grounds for investigations of ghosts and poltergeists, many being very old and steeped in a long, eventful and often bloody history. They were once called taverns or alehouses and were frequented by prostitutes, criminals, thieves, vagabonds, gamblers and soldiers; all of them just out for a good time and a quick profit. Old inns were often used as courthouses, brothels and gambling dens. With this combustible mixture of contradictory elements, it's no wonder many of our popular drinking dens are haunted.

The Brazz (Le Bistro de la Gare), The Enterprise Centre, Eastbourne

The Brazz, a fine bistro at The Enterprise Centre has strange Victorian ghosts. The venue is in a former railway-shunting depot, dates from 1860 and still has its original timber roof. It was here that a man was killed in an accident. Although no one knows the precise details about the accident, Alex Killik says she often sees his ghostly apparition late at night, together with his young assistant.

The Brazz, since it is situated on the upper storey of the former depot, has a set of steps from the street leading to a door directly into the bistro. In Victorian times, the depot below was a holding centre for mail and baggage. The trains actually shunted right into the premises to deliver the mailbags – so the accident that killed the unfortunate man probably happened right under their roof.

From time to time, an alarm sounds and the door swings open and there is a sudden freezing over of the temperature in the bar. Alex, and her husband Peter are now used to seeing two people standing in the doorway in Victorian working clothes; the ghosts of an engine driver and, beside him, a small boy carrying a coal scuttle. Their faces are sweaty and blackened from their labours in the engine room of an old steam engine.

The Golden Galleon, Seaford

Located in a beautiful location at the Exceat Bridge over the River Cuckmere in Seaford, with panoramic views over marshland, it's no surprise The Golden Galleon's ghost is connected to the smuggling fraternity. In the middle ages, Seaford was one of the main ports for Southern England and the River Cuckmere was used for transporting illicit goods until raids by the French and the silting up of the harbour changed its fortunes The young barmaid, Cassie, whose parents have run the pub for the past twenty years, says that many years ago, a man who was acting as night lookout for smugglers was apprehended and brutally murdered by the revenue men. When Cassie's parents took over the pub, the family heard how the murdered man's restless ghost had haunted the bars, spooking out the previous owners who had lived on the premises. Since Cassie and her family have taken over, no further sightings have been reported.

The Golden Galleon pub

The River Cuckmere from Exceat Bridge

The Lamb Inn, 36 High Street, Old Town, Eastbourne

With its oldest parts dating from the twelfth century, The Lamb in Eastbourne is located next door to the old Church of St. Mary. An underground tunnel runs from The Lamb into the Church (although in some accounts, it's claimed to run to the Parsonage) and was once used by smugglers to transport their loot to its hiding place. Its entrance can still be seen. The tunnel is supposed to be haunted by the ghost of a White Lady. There's also a priest's hole in the cellars, and a gloomy vaulted crypt, which may have been used as an underground chapel or even a burial vault. It is thick with dankness and horribly oppressive and staff are afraid to go down there alone. The remains of a Roman boat have been discovered nearby during redevelopment.

The pub has the distinction of having been visited by the popular TV programme *Most Haunted*. 'Loads of orbs were detected,' say the bar staff. Further back, in 1852, a Dr. Darling gave a lecture about spiritualism at The Lamb. But his audience took fright and ran away – as a most terrible clap of thunder crashed down from the heavens.

But one of the strangest stories is that of a little boy who walked to school with his mother, passing the pub on their way. 'They have horses there, don't they?' he said his mother. It transpired the child could see, around the side of the pub where the garages are, exactly the way it was centuries ago. There were stables, clearly visible to the small boy although not to anyone else. 'I used to work there,' he told his mother. 'I looked after those garages when there were once horses inside. I looked after *that* horse, over *there*' he added, pointing, but his mother could only see how the sideway was now,

Above: The Lamb Inn

Right: Through the arch of the old
vaulted chamber

Vaulted Crypt, ceiling detail

The Priest's Hole – a place to hide from the soldiers during the Reformation

with parked cars and garages. Shortly after, she paid a visit to the pub and explained to the amazed staff what her little boy had told her. Everything checked out. There were, indeed, once stables where the garages now stand and there was no possible way the small boy could have known the history of the buildings in such detail.

There's also a tall, male ghost, who resembles a person of around forty-years-old with blond curly hair. One of the barmaids says that as she's looking around, she glimpses his shade out of the corner of her eye. Sometimes she turns around to say 'Hi' but suddenly, he is no longer there. 'But he's not hostile,' she adds. She is used to him now as he appears regularly when the pub is empty, as though wanting to keep her company. Also, an old man is sometimes seen sitting in a chair in the back bar.

'All the ghosts here are happy spirits except for just one,' says one of the barmaids. She explains how, four years ago, a laundry room at the top of the building caught fire. No explanation could be found by experts about how the blaze started. The owners were still on the premises otherwise the people on the top floor would have died in the fire. 'But fortunately all the bad spirits went away in the fire,' continues the barmaid. 'Only good spirits are left.' Then she adds, 'Sometimes a little girl has been heard by several people, crying in the laundry room. There's also an old doll's house and there's definitely something weird about it although we can't decide what it is. Perhaps the dolls' house once belonged to the little girl ghost.'

The sideway with garages where once there were stables.

All of the Lamb Inn's bar staff agree about one thing. 'All the spirits left downstairs are good. Their energy is all soaked up in the walls, but it's a happy energy,' they say. They explain how two prostitutes once lived and worked upstairs when the inn was used as a brothel and they are reputed to haunt the building to this day. They are kindly, ethereal beings and have stayed around to look after the child ghosts. Let's hope, one day, they manage to console the weeping little girl and help her to move on.

The Lamb Inn is the oldest hostelry in Britain, according to the excellent website www.kwackers.com/eastbourne. It provided a service as a stopping place for the London stage coach and was also used by mendicant friars and pilgrims on their way to worship at a shrine in Chichester.

The Prince Albert, 9 High Street, Old Town, Eastbourne

'The female bar staff are always complaining there's something very creepy going on in the ladies' loo,' says Terry, the owner of the Prince Albert. 'On more than one occasion, women have said something has brushed past them in there.'

When several people all report the same experience, it seems there must be something really spooky going on. What is known is that the pub, which originally dated from

The Prince Albert

around 1910, was 'pushed back' to accommodate the widening of the road in 1935 and most of the original building had to be sacrificed although there are still some older part in existence. Could it be this disturbance has antagonised a displaced spirit into making its presence known?

Royal Oak and Castle, The Market Square, Pevensey

Right outside the Royal Oak and Castle pub, according to the *Eastbourne Herald* dated 25 October 2007, is the spot where the 1399 siege defender Lady Joan Pelham is said to still be trying to repel the army of Richard II. (Please see separate story under Chapter 13, 'Paranormal Pevensey'). On the night of a paranormal investigation, the landlord, Brian Smart, said, 'We shall go out into the castle grounds late at night. Many people have had weird experiences.' One such person was Charlie Prangnell, who moved to the pub with his family when he was about fifteen years old in the mid sixties:

Charlie's family took over the pub from a lady called Mrs. Chapman whose husband had died, and they decided to keep the former landlady on. Parts of the building were derelict as they hadn't been lived in for around fifteen years. The Prangnell family set about decorating it – most of the bedrooms had adjoining doors so they had to put a passageway all the way through. The lounge, which was upstairs, seemed to attract a lot of paranormal activity. Many people who went there claimed, quite independently, that there was someone outside the door. It seemed they had heard the phantom footsteps. Several people who'd been distressed for some reason, and rushed to the bathroom, claimed they felt a comforting arm go around their shoulders.

'The room always had a strange perfumed smell,' says Charlie. 'It didn't matter what we did to get rid of it; it was always there. It was Mrs. Chapman's room and she stayed there until she died.' Mrs. Chapman had a way of walking very heavily on one leg, due to an immobility problem, and Charlie could always hear her, the awkward gait and the heavy tread.

Some time after Mrs. Chapman died, Charlie's sister moved into the room. She complained to Charlie that, while she was doing her friend's hair, she saw something slide across the dressing table and heard the sound of tapping. To stop her worrying, Charlie said the tapping was down to him working in the garage. But when he went to bed himself that night, he was awoken to the sound of the unmistakeable footsteps, one light, one heavy, trudging outside his door. He could only assume it was Mrs. Chapman's ghost moving along the corridor.

Charlie had yet one more scary experience in The Royal Oak. His stepbrother moved from another room into Charlie's old room, so Charlie found himself relegated to one of the rooms that hadn't been used for over fifteen years. He returned to his bedroom late one night and snuggled down into his bed. Suddenly a heavy weight was pressing down on his legs. At the time he had his eyes closed, so he kept them that way, feeling too scared to open them and face what was on top of him. He remembered nothing after that, but the experience didn't have a lasting impression on him; for some strange reason, he says, he lost his fear of the ghosts of the Royal Oak.

The Royal Oak and Castle, main entrance

The Royal Oak and Castle, side view

In the main bar, several people saw a shadow cross the area, while others claimed to have seen a ghost coming out of Charlie's room.

Jessica, who is the current manager of The Royal Oak, tells of her recent, disturbing experience in the cellar, where she saw some wine on the floor near the door. She leaned over to pick it up, and then she sensed there was someone – or something – in the cold area where the beer is kept. The door to the area was open, so Jessica, feeling scared, tried to close it. 'But I felt sure someone or something helped me to close that door,' she says. 'It was as though there was a force from the other side, pulling at the door as I was trying to close it.' Jessica didn't wait to find out; instead she scooted upstairs, trying to convince herself that the landlord, Brian, was 'acting stupid and playing a joke on me.' But she found Brian was upstairs and could not have been responsible for the activity in the beer area.

'I never went down there again,' says Jessica, shivering.

Once, Brian decided to swap his bedroom to another room, and, like Charlie Prangnell, he, too, had a very weird experience. The first night he slept in the new room, he felt something tugging hard at his duvet, as though trying to wake him up.

Royal Sovereign, 12 Seaside Road, Eastbourne

The Royal Sovereign was once a police station, a fact celebrated by the panel in the four corners of every window, displaying a police badge, (see image). It might also explain the appearance of the Royal Sovereign's resident ghost, which haunts the ground floor, including the bar and kitchen. Although it is shadowy, it is described as always wearing a 'big tall hat'.

The Royal Sovereign dates from around the late eighteen hundreds. Its ghost has been witnessed by a customer (who has named it 'Harry') and by the cleaners, including one who has on occasion taken her little son to work with her. One day, the cleaner heard her son 'chatting away' to someone in the kitchen while she was busy at her duties. 'Who were you talking to, Jack?' she asked him. 'Oh, that man in the big tall hat,' the little boy replied. The little boy was completely comfortable with his shadowy friend and saw nothing at all strange in their rather one-sided conversations.

The customer, known as 'Vinnie' witnessed the shadowy figure moving from the bar area across to the section at the rear of the pub housing the pool table. There have been other instances of poltergeist activity, for example, people have been shoved and poked in the arm and when they turn around, there's no one there. Glasses have been dashed off the shelf. Of course, this might be due to an entirely separate entity – or else the former policeman, claimed to be the source of this apparition, was not a worthy representation of the law!

'I don't think ghosts ever mean to harm you,' says one of the barmaids, a relief worker for the owners who were on holiday at the time of writing. 'I think they are just people who have died but are not yet at peace. I definitely believe that there is an after-life.'

The first policemen, known as 'peelers' after Sir Robert Peel who masterminded the new force for law and order, began to watch over the streets of London in 1829. Early

The Royal Sovereign

The Royal Sovereign's police badge window panel

police headgear was virtually just a top hat. The police incorporated the traditional high bobby's helmet into their uniform in 1863. The police badge, a sixteen or eight-pointed star, is a representation of the Star of Brunswick, an image taken from the German feudal state, Braunschweig, once ruled over by the British Hanoverian kings, from George I to William IV.

Early police carried a wooden truncheon, secured within their blue tailcoats, and wooden rattle to sound the alarm. The latter was replaced in 1880 by the whistle.

The Smugglers Inn, High Street, Pevensey

The Smugglers, High Street, Pevensey dates from 1527 and is a short distance from Pevensey Castle. A ghost has been reported and it takes the form of a mysterious grey lady who glides through walls, according to the *Eastbourne Herald* dated 25 October 2007. She is said to be a benevolent spirit. One landlord claimed that after he locked up for the night, he heard a sudden loud bang on the door. He went to check and found, to his amazement, that the door was no longer bolted.

There were, and still are, some pretty weird things going on in this ancient pub. At the time, the landlady Tania Messom told the *Eastbourne Herald* reporter, 'We are

The Smugglers. A young girl hanged herself in the dormer room on the east side, (to the left of the pub's roadside elevation).

Above: The dormer window

Left: The garage, once the location of the old fire station

having to warn everyone that when they talk to a ghost, they should gently touch them. If their hand goes right through – worry!' Also reported was a poltergeist, which 'stamps' heavily on the floorboards and turns the light switches on and off.

Current landlady Sue reports something walking across the bar and through the door leading to the restaurant and is certain this was the ghost. Husband Stewart explains that around two hundred years ago, a young girl hanged herself upstairs in the end room on the east side of the pub (the roof's dormer window to the left of the pub's roadside elevation). Her tragic act is commonly thought to have been due to a disappointment in love. She sounds too young to be the mysterious lady in grey, so perhaps there are two female ghosts haunting the pub interior.

Around the early 1900s, the rear of the building where the garage stands was used as a fire station and people have subsequently seen the phantom of an old fireman in the area. 'Also, people have taken photographs around the pub, and images have appeared in them of figures that weren't there when they were taken,' says Stewart. 'When people have taken photographs of the pub – there are often phantoms floating overhead!'

Paranormal phenomena often appears photos, although the photographers claim there was no one else there at the time. Frequently, these additional images can take the form of orbs. Many thousands of people all over the world have reported discovering these spheres of light in their digital images and some believe they these are beings from another dimension. In other words, there could be a parallel world existing alongside our own reality that we cannot normally perceive. Whether this is the same as the concept we call 'the other side', ie. a world inhabited by our traditional ghosts and spirits – or an entirely separate concept - we cannot know for certain. But clearly, it is illogical to believe that just because we can't see something, it isn't there, even if we can't actually prove that it is.

Stewart also tells how around twenty-five years ago, the wire used to slice the cheese kept disappearing and no one could understand why – another weird happening that is impossible to explain by any rational means.

Author's note:
While researching at The Smugglers Inn, I was given a lead for a photograph for one of my other haunted stories in the area. After taking the shot, I returned, just to make sure I had photographed the right building. But things weren't as I'd left them a half hour earlier. The draught beer dispenser had 'given up the ghost' – excuse the pun – and pulling a pint was proving painful. And then – to make matters worse, the till had gone bananas and the customer couldn't get his change.

When the barmaid, turned to me and said, 'It's you. You've spooked the place!' – even though she was smiling - I thought it was time to beat a hasty retreat and catch the first bus out of town.

The Star Inn, High Street, Alfriston

Some years ago, a woman in a modern gown was said to have terrified the servants at The Star Inn. Presumably the gown was modern at that time, when the pub had servants, but probably wouldn't be to us today. On two occasions, it's reported, the

The Star Inn

The Star Inn's window star

servants flatly refused to stay on the premises. There are two other ghosts claimed to haunt this pub. One wears a medieval court costume, while another looks like a Victorian farmer, and he sits directly under the wall clock in the lounge. One landlord, it is claimed, woke unexpectedly one night and he saw the phantom farmer, whom he described as about sixty years old, dressed in a pleated smock, leggings tied with string and a floppy hat, walk across his bedroom. The phantom gazed at the wall and then just turned around and went back where he'd come from.

Guests have been reported being locked in their rooms by someone or something paranormal. They had to use the internal telephone system to notify the staff of their plight.

An article in the *Eastbourne Herald* dated 11 November 2008 entitled: 'Spooky goings-on at an Alfriston pub' details an investigation by medium, Michael Kingscote. The event was a radio show for Sovereign Radio in celebration of Hallowe'en. Michael and partner Kim went with the team and Kim took a photograph, in the presence of Michael himself and the manager, Cherrill Starmer. Later, on looking at the image, the amazed team discovered a man there, in the background, who Michael claimed, was not there at the time it was taken. The photograph seemed to be a reflected image bounced off a one-way glass into an office, which makes sense as ghosts, it is believed, use light to create form.

Michael was determined to investigate with an open mind. 'But I found this place to be one of the most active,' he said. Paranormal activity at the pub was so impressive that Michael actually began to question whether his equipment could be malfunctioning. For example, in the heritage room, which was the main area for study, footsteps were heard above although they knew there was no one there. But it was the photograph that Michael found the most convincing evidence. 'I have never had anything that appears so clear,' said Michael. 'I have highlighted it for clarity, but it looks like a priest and there's an arm stroking his face. From the angle the arm would have to be lying down.' Then Michael, Kim and Sharon from Sovereign Radio all heard a heavy moan, although Michael was alone and the others were downstairs. Yet, they all heard the strange noise simultaneously. Cherrill listed a number of other incidents that had occurred prior to the investigation.

- A housekeeper was pushed out of one of the rooms although there was no one else there.
- A glass of wine fell off a table. No one was anywhere near at the time.
- While at the bar, Cherrill's husband brought her a drink. There was already a drink on the edge of a round table and her husband placed her glass in the middle of the table. To the amazement of Cherrill, her husband and a barmaid, the glass suddenly moved across the table and smashed onto the floor. In spite of the floor being carpeted, which should have cushioned the impact, the glass smashed into thousands of pieces.
- A thermometer was placed in various parts of the room. The temperature fluctuated, suddenly becoming extremely cold, then rising again, a sure sign of a ghostly presence. Luckily the ghosts (or poltergeists) did no real harm and seemed to be friendly.

It's also believed that King Alfred the Great, who allegedly lived in his Palace at nearby West Dean, actually burnt his cakes at The Star Inn, while he was distracted planning his battle strategy against the ferocious Danes. However, the county of Somerset also lays claim to a similar story involving a swineherd's hut where Alfred took shelter and got scolded by the swineherd's wife for his reprehensible culinary skills. However, The Star is sticking to its own version of events.

Dating from around the thirteenth century, the Inn was known as The Star of Bethlehem until 1520, when it was once run by monks from Battle Abbey, offering a place to stay to pilgrims and friars who were travelling to the Shrine of St. Richard at Chichester.

The Tally Ho, 42 Church Street, Old Town, Eastbourne

'The trouble with our ghost is that she talks incessantly,' says Lis, the landlady of The Tally Ho. 'We only moved in two weeks ago, but we heard all about it from the previous landlord. We are looking forward to meeting our ghost. The previous landlord said we would be sure to see her soon.'

The Tally Ho has a sociable little ghost

They used to say children should be seen and not heard, but, according to the reports, the reverse is true in the case of this precocious ghost of a ten-year-old, who is much more verbal than she is visible. One young woman who lived in an upstairs room was actually tapped on the shoulder in the night to get her attention, and then the little girl ghost immediately started chattering away to her. The little girl has been sighted in several places, sometimes sitting in a corner, sometimes wandering along a corridor and just once – actually in the bar.

There's also a very old doll, discovered in a box in the junk room, and it's possible this may have belonged to the child ghost. It does seem to present some sort of evidence that a female child once lived in the building. Lis says she firmly believes in ghosts, as she was convinced there was a child ghost in a previous pub she managed.

There's another paranormal event that happens regularly and is verified by the Tally Ho chef, Jim, who also worked at the pub before Lis and her husband took it over. The staff were told never to move a certain picture in one of the front bedrooms, where staff once lived many years ago. It's a very old picture of a middle-aged couple, and if it's moved, or turned around, the next day it's found replaced exactly as it was in the first instance. So it might just as well be left where it is because that's where 'whatever moves it' wants it to hang!

The Tiger Inn, The Green, East Dean

It is claimed that The Tiger Inn is haunted by a mysterious White Lady with a fascinating past. Stuart and Jo Crook manage this late seventeenth century inn in the quaint old village of East Dean. They explain that the White Lady has been around for several hundred years, in fact, since the time of the Great Plague. Late at night, staff can hear doors banging and windows slamming and sometimes pictures suddenly fall off the wall.

Stuart believes the White Lady once worked for the Davies-Gilbert estate, one of the two major founding families responsible for Eastbourne. The Davies-Gilbert family owned the village of East Dean and the Estate as well as a large swathe of land in the area and employed a great number of people, especially as farmers and farm-labourers. A lady who lives next door to the pub remembers having seen and heard the White Lady from since she was a small child.

So why does the White Lady still show herself? Stuart tells how the three terraced cottages adjacent to the inn were a hospital during Napoleonic times. People who fled the plague in the towns and cities came to the area by boat, to seek safety from the disease. Some of them were treated in the hospital. It's believed the White Lady was once a nurse in the hospital, and so severely traumatised by her experiences there that she is unable to move on.

The inn got its name from a tiger gracing the coat of arms of a local lord, but although it was identified as a puma, the pub retained its original name, The Tiger.

The seventeenth-century Tiger Inn

The Tiger Inn Signboard

These cottages were once a hospital that treated plague victims

The Wheatsheaf Inn 2 Church Street, Willingdon, Eastbourne

It's not really done to go into the pub, then use the facilities with impunity and not buy a drink. So, three years ago, staff at the quaint old village pub, The Wheatsheaf, were amazed to see the ghosts of two old ladies, sitting in a corner of the bar and just chatting to each other. When approached, the talkative twosome disappeared. Later, in March 2009, the BBC News channel reported that Martin, the landlord, had implemented new 'novelty taps' and an honesty box, so customers could serve themselves when the pub was busy. But it seems unlikely the ghosts will be too impressed with that!

Although no one seems to have seen the two old ladies recently, the latest news is that the ghosts are still around in this seventeenth-century pub, which was originally two cottages and part of the Willingdon Estate. James, the second chef, says he hasn't seen anything himself but that several people have reported an elderly man with a flat cap walking to and fro in the downstairs bar.

James pointed out the handles beneath one of the tables in the restaurant section of the pub. 'It's a laying out table,' he said. 'They used to put dead people on this to get them ready for burial.'

Maybe the man in the flat cap was once laid out on this table!

Another member of the bar staff, Leah Hughes, explains that although the back half of the pub is a newish addition, the front is very old, probably four or five hundred

The Wheatsheaf

James, the Wheatsheaf's second chef, seated at the 'laying-out' table in the Wheatsheaf's restaurant area

years. It's here she once heard a persistent knocking while she was alone in the bar. (Leah's dad lives upstairs so she spends quite a lot of time here.) Leah looked around but could see nothing. So she sat with her back pressed hard against the wall.

'Another thing I don't like, besides the knocking,' says Leah, 'is the whispering. There are lots of whispers and it really scares me. My dad doesn't believe in it all, but then, *he* hasn't heard the knocking and the whispers.'

Ye Olde Smugglers Inne, Waterloo Square, Alfriston

In 1994, the owner of this pub claimed to see a phantom woman at the base of the stairs. She was wearing modern clothes and may have been a former landlady who was unhappy about being ousted by the new incumbents. Of course, it's claimed this sometimes happens to people who haven't moved on and don't realise they are actually dead. Sometimes their hostile energy persuades the new occupants to move at the first opportunity. Also reported is a seafaring gentleman and also a phantom who might be a farmer or a shepherd.

There is still, it appears, considerable paranormal activity in this quaint old inn, whose original parts date from 1358 while additions to the structure date from around the sixteenth century. Dixie, a young barmaid currently working at the inn, says she

Ye Olde Smugglers Inne, Alfriston

frequently gets 'the shivers' as she feels the presences around her. She hasn't seen the phantom woman mentioned above, but there has been a male phantom who moves 'up and down across the bar area' right in front of her eyes. On one side of the bar area, there's a large shelf covered in relics, weapons and old kitchen utensils and cooking tools and implements, etc. Sometimes, without warning, one of these items simply falls off the shelf. 'This pub is very *very* haunted,' says Dixie firmly,' 'especially the older parts.'

Ye Olde Smugglers Inne was originally called The Market Cross Inn. Later it was renamed because of the energetic activities of the local Alfriston gang. Dixie says the gang's leader, Stanton Collins' was left the house by his butcher father and he ran The Market House as a butcher's shop. In the 1820s, it became a haunt for his smuggling activities. Church wardens were tenants between 1827 and 1831 when The Market Cross was run as an almshouse for parish paupers. Stanton Collins eventually paid the price for his criminal activities. He was responsible for shoving an excise man off the cliff, but ended up getting seven years' transportation for sheep-stealing in 1831. The staff think the male phantom sighted by Dixie, among others, may actually be the ghost of Stanton Collins.

The present name of Ye Olde Smugglers Inne dates from around the 1920s. It's said there are lots of ghost stories related to this pub. But it's also possible the smugglers invented stories about hauntings around the Inn – a common ploy of the gangs to scare people away and keep their contraband safe from discovery – and from the dreaded excise men.

CHAPTER 7

THE GHOSTS OF DEANS PLACE HOTEL

Not much can be kept secret in a hotel. So, it seems, hotels can be a great source of ghost stories, especially buildings with a long history that has generated some mysterious and intriguing tales – and plenty of guests to witness the ensuing phenomena. One such place is the imposing Deans Place Hotel.

Deans Place Hotel, Alfriston

Deans Place Hotel, is located in the fourteenth century village of Alfriston near Eastbourne. This one-time farming estate became a private hotel in the early twentieth century. Previously it has been used as a farmhouse, a hospital and, further back, it was even the local pest house.

Mr. Richard Gardner, who was operations manager for Deans Place Hotel three year ago, tells of a female ghost who scared staff and guests out of their wits. She is the manifestation of an unfortunate woman in fear of her life, who was standing at the top of a flight of stairs as they were engulfed by flames. The stairs are no longer there, but the female ghost is occasionally seen hovering around in thin air, as though preparing herself to be consumed by the raging fire.

The hotel is also claimed to be haunted by a lady in a very posh blue silk dress. In his book *Haunted Inns of Sussex*, the writer, Roger Long, mentions a a story about a young girl who was staying at the hotel. As she was coming downstairs, she was brushed aside rather brusquely by a figure of a youngish woman in a blue gown. Vexed, she went to find a member of staff to complain about the woman's rudeness, but she was informed that there was no one staying at the hotel of that description.

One of the most famous stories about the blue-gowned ghost is that of a maid who was washing up in the kitchen when she heard a knock on the door. She said, 'Come in,' and then a lady in a blue dress of expensive silk entered the room, before suddenly disappearing. Later, during renovations in the early 1900s, a female skeleton was discovered beneath the floor – was this the human remains of the lady in blue? Roger Long suggests she may have died violently, otherwise what was the point in concealing the body under the floor?

According to Judy Middleton in her *Ghosts of Sussex*, the discovery of the bones did not stop the manifestations. The phantom lady was subsequently seen by several guests. A more recent incident, said to have occurred in the 1960s, involved a Mrs. Saddler and her little daughter. One evening, the girl, aged five years, said a lady in a blue dress had passed her on her way back from the bathroom. Knowing how kids can imagine things, her mum took little notice. Then, the next morning, the child asked the staff about the lady and it transpired many people had witnessed this ghost, claimed to be that of a woman who was brutally murdered many years ago. In this version, her remains were dissected and hidden in a settle.

No one knows who she was or the date of her death, in fact, Roger Long stated that scientists had been unable to date the skeleton. People say she is a benign ghost although there is something 'not quite right' about her. She never makes a sound and is surrounded by a freezing temperature.

There is another claim, although this may be the only sighting – that the misty figure of a young boy has appeared at the doorway to a bedroom as recorded by Andrew Green on www.mystical.co.uk.

More Deans Place Ghosts:

- Dixie, the young barmaid at the nearby Ye Olde Smugglers Inne, tells a story of how a couple who stayed at the hotel had a scary experience. They said they looked

Deans Place Hotel, Alfriston

out of their window and very clearly saw a horrible black phantom in the garden. 'That hotel is very *very* haunted,' says Dixie.

- One particularly sinister apparition is that of a disembodied hand covered in jewels.
- The ghost of a man in a tall hat and white coat has also been seen in the attic.
- Outside, in the car park, a ghost dog is said to prowl.

The Village Pest House

During the eighteenth and nineteenth centuries the village pest house was located in the grounds of Deans Place, where people afflicted with infectious diseases were sent to recover – or not as the case may be. It was, of course, essential to isolate them from society. A pest house must have been a horrific place and it is easy to imagine how traumatised these people must have been. Perhaps some of the hauntings may even be attributed to the pest house patients.

CHAPTER 8

YE OLDE BAKERY'S PHANTOM BLACK WITCH

Situated at 25 Seaside Road, Eastbourne, Ye Olde Bakery continues in its tradition of supplying delicious fare for the traveller and passer-by. Dating back to 1790, this attractive old building has its own fascinating history – and its own special ghost. But this is a ghost with some very distinctive qualities.

The building operated from the late eighteenth century to the latter part of the 1920s as a bakery, and now is run as a restaurant by Mrs. Margaret Mander and her husband. She says that in its early life, the rear of the building, that is the part closest to the sea, served a special purpose. Fishermen's nets were hung out to dry on the mezzanine ceiling. Also people sold fish from that rear, seafront position so the whole building and its surroundings must have been bustling with marine-type activity. The original baking coal oven was installed in 1850 (see image, with *real* bread!) although now the bread is baked by gas.

Ye Olde Bakery's female ghost is claimed to have been a witch. This was a weird old lady who always dressed in black and terrified the local children. Margaret wasn't able to accurately date her physical lifetime at the bakery, but it's claimed she sold lobsters outside the front door. Whether or not she really *was* a witch, or whether this was just the children's imaginations working overtime, isn't clear. Whoever she was, her ghostly presence is still strongly felt in the building and some people say they wouldn't want to risk staying there overnight.

A large number of staff, past and present, have reported a spooky atmosphere and, over the years, the former bakery has been visited by people with psychic abilities, all of whom have picked up the presence of the little witchy phantom lady dressed in black. But, fortunately, most people say that there is nothing bad to be detected in the building, a fact confirmed by Margaret.

'We know she is completely harmless,' says Margaret. 'We have been here for six years and we have never had any problem with her. We've never made any big changes apart from some light decorating, so we haven't disturbed her at all.' This, of course, is important as departed spirits dislike it if the place they formerly lived in is changed around. They become indignant and start acting up, not considering they should have moved over and allowed the new incumbents their space. Sometimes though, it seems the Olde Bakery's witchy lady ghost just wants to remind them she is still around. 'Every now and again a door bangs, for no apparent reason,' says Margaret. 'But we know exactly who it is.'

Left: Ye Olde Bakery, front elevation

Below: Ye Olde Bakery, side elevation

Bread just baked – Ye Olde Bakery

Margaret explains that the upstairs part of the building is very small. Occasionally, when especially busy, she and her husband have stayed there overnight although most of the time they go home to sleep. Either way, when they go down in the morning, or return to work from their home, they find certain items of equipment have been turned on, for example, the till light and the dishwasher, even though they know for certain everything has been switched off and closed down properly the night before.

One interesting fact about witches is that they used to hold special rituals to deter French invaders from landing on our coast. Maybe the Olde Bakery's witch-ghost was a part of this tradition during her lifetime. Perhaps what we hear about witches through the ages always being considered 'evil' is not entirely true – certainly, it seems, in Eastbourne their powers were sometimes used to repel the French enemy – for the good of all.

CHAPTER 9

CHURCHES, BURIAL GROUNDS AND SACRED PLACES

There's a lot of folklore surrounding churches, being as they are, and even more so in past times, the central focus of a community. There used to be a strong belief that the first corpse buried in a new burial ground belonged to the Devil. So wealthy people got around this by arranging for a so-called 'nobody', say a tramp or a servant, to be the first body interred. After that, they would be confident in burying their own dead in the new graveyard.

Roads from far locations to churches were usually laid out in straight lines to facilitate the passage of coffins to their final resting place.

The Moving Church in Alfriston

When the foundations were being laid for what is now the imposing Parish Church of St. Andrews, and the beginnings of walls began to appear above them, something truly bizarre happened. The workmen left that night, after their labours, and on returning the next morning they were utterly bewildered to find the stones had disappeared and the field, a piece of land west of the main street, was empty. They searched high and low for the missing materials and discovered them lying in a field to the east, at a place called The Tye. So they lumped and heaved the stones back to where they'd been originally placed.

Imagine their consternation when, the following night, exactly the same thing happened. So it was decided that this was where they would build the church. Here the church remains, but no one knew if this shifting of the building materials was God's work, or an act of the Devil. Then, one day, four white oxen were discovered lying together in the shape of a cross, their rumps on the inside, their heads on the outside. This is why the church is now shaped like a cruciform.

However, this story is not specific to St. Andrews. Similar legends are claimed for other churches in other places. But we have to remember that the power of deities is far-reaching and all-embracing and is certainly not confined to Alfriston!

The Parish Church of St. Andrews

Miracles

The Parish Church of St. Andrews lies on a former Saxon Burial ground. According to the village website, a Christian virgin, St. Lewinna, was killed by Saxons in 690 AD. Her body lay in the church and her relics are claimed to have created several miracles, at least, until they were stolen by a Belgian monk who removed them to the Priory St. Winox in 1058.

The Clergy House

The fourteenth century priest's house with its timber frames and thatched roof was built in the mid thirteen hundreds and can be located close to the Parish Church of St. Andrews. In her book, *Sussex Haunted Heritage*, Debra Munn tells how custodian Nick Jarvis and volunteer Shelley Bernard used to smell the odour of a cigar early in the mornings around the house during the 1990s – and what was worse: smoking was *banned* around the property. They believed it was a nobleman from a past century and his invisible presence was strongly felt by Shelley Bernard and sent shivers down her spine. Staff also heard footsteps above them when the house was closed to visitors and a receptionist named Jack saw a male apparition in the Hall, wearing the clothing of a customs and excise man, complete with sword, big boots and black cloak.

The old Clergy House at Alfriston

'He looked like a real flesh-and-blood human being,' Jack is quoted as saying. 'His face didn't change and he didn't appear to notice me.' The apparition eventually disappeared through a pillar. What seems to have been agreed by all eyewitnesses is that the phantom was most definitely male. Jack also recounted another strange phenomenon, a phantom smuggler's barge wending its way upriver in the mist at high tide. There were phantom voices and a phantom dog barking – all very spooky!

There has also been some poltergeist activity reported, for example, items being stolen away and then reappearing, napkins suddenly landing on the floor for no apparent reason, books falling off shelves. Debra Munn says she herself experienced the latter phenomenon in May 1997; as she went to pay for a book, another large book fell off the shelf above and landed beside her on the floor.

A Threadbare Old Man

A building near the Church in Alfriston was, in 1350, the home of a parish priest. It's claimed to be haunted by a poor old man in threadbare grey clothing who also once lived there. However, once the building was renovated, the sightings stopped.

The Disappearing Nun

The All Saints Convalescent Hospital at The Meads in Eastbourne was once run by an order of nuns, the Sisters of the Poor, from 1869 to 1959 under Mother Superior, Harriet Brownlow Byron. This might explain the strange story of a senior cook, who in September, 1975, encountered the shade of a middle-aged grey nun. Then the nun suddenly disappeared, rather dramatically, in a puff of smoke. All Saints Convalescent Hospital is, again, changing use – into a flat conversion.

Heavy Rock in the Nunnery

A former Eastbourne nunnery The Chapel in Belmore Road, was converted into a garage and subsequently became a studio just three months prior to a haunting in 2002. The venue freaked out a band of heavy rockers, according to *The Argus* dated 19 February. *Cobra*, a group of four musicians, was convinced their spooks were nuns who objected to what they saw as 'the Devil's music.'

Clive Rogers, a guitarist, defended the music. 'There is nothing nasty or unpleasant about our music. It's just no-nonsense new classic rock. But every time we crank up the volume and really get things moving, we can heard these female voices singing hymns.' The band found the intervention very spooky, and explained it seemed to occur mostly when they were really belting out their stuff.

The venue, a brick-built building, was a nunnery at the turn of the twentieth century, with a cobbled yard where horses were tethered. A number of other bands used the studio, but only Cobra's music seemed to affect the nuns who always tried to overpower it with their own shrill choral singing. Studio owner, Vince Von Bastrum said, 'It's very bizarre. It's a high-pitched sound which can be heard over the band, no matter how loud they play.' He points out that it never happened with other clients who played more relaxed music. 'It's just Cobra's rock that seems to set it off.'

Vince added that he was planning to move into a flat above the studio, but his girlfriend was reluctant and insisted she would not go near the place if it is haunted.

A Musical Poltergeist in Polegate Rectory

Polegate is located around 8 km north of Eastbourne and its old rectory in Church Road is claimed by its owner to be haunted – people enter and 'see things'. The front doors shake violently for no apparent reason and phantom footsteps have been heard around the area of the piano.

CHAPTER 10

MICHELHAM PRIORY – A MAGNET FOR THE PARANORMAL

Founded in 1229 by Gilbert de Aquila III, Earl of Pembroke, Michelham Priory in Upper Dicker belonged to an Augustinian religious order known as the 'black canons' until its dissolution in 1637, instigated by Henry VIII in his mission to crush his Roman Catholic enemies. Around this time, the Priory passed into private ownership, although other accounts claim an earlier date – that it was sold to Thomas Sackville in 1601 whose family owned it for almost 300 years before being passed on to several further owners.

The Priory also has a history of witchcraft, a fact supported by the discovery in 1927 of stone Bellarmine jars from the seventeenth century in which ingredients for spells – or curses - were sometimes placed by witches. Sometimes a witch would bury a jar near to their target, with something ghastly inside – maybe an animal's heart or a dead baby. This was not, of course, the original purpose of the jars, which were produced, innocently enough, for the storage of beer or wine and which bore a sculpture of a theologian of the sixteenth century, Cardinal Roberto Bellarmino.

Michelham Priory, it is claimed, is haunted by a number of ghosts, including, according to Debra Munn in *Sussex Haunted Heritage,* the ghost of King Harold hastening to confront William the Conqueror at Battle in 1066. However, Debra Munn points out that King Harold died over one hundred and fifty years before the Priory was built on the earlier site of a manor house. Much later, in the fifteenth century and prior to its dissolution, the Priory went through a sticky patch, falling into a decline brought about by some irresponsible canons who thought nothing of getting blind drunk in local taverns and ignoring their religious rituals. Debra Munn cites one who even had an illicit affair with a local woman. Such a colourful history is bound to leave a few ghosts behind.

One of the hauntings is attributed to a former Canon, as explained by David Scanlan in his book *Paranormal Sussex* published by Amberley. In 2004, David investigated Michelham Priory with a team from the Hampshire Ghost Club. He says, 'I had a very unusual encounter here. Coming through the main entrance, just past the undercroft, I was confronted by the ghost of a brown-clad monk standing at the foot of a staircase. The monk raised his right hand and pointed upstairs. He then shouted in a very loud voice, 'He is a ******* sick bastard!' After this, the monk vanished and David says that immediately after the incident, another team member entered, but unfortunately, he was too late to see anything. Another visitor claims to have seen a monk by the Gatehouse, but whether this is the same monk as the one witnessed by David at the main entrance, is not certain.

The Terrified Horses

In 1927 a fire raged through the Priory and burnt down the Tudor farmhouse. It terrified the horses in their stables. At the time, the Priory had been sold to a Mr. Beresford Wright, who discovered the fire himself. Staff who looked after the horses were alarmed to find the animals still scared and kicking at their stable walls four days later. Mr. Beresford Wright was most concerned when he was summoned to the stables to see for himself how the horses were still shaking with terror and covered with sweat. A few more weeks went by and the property's owner was even more amazed to find that the beasts had still not settled.

Then he found out the reason why the horses were still so badly scared. A stable boy informed him that the horses were frightened of the 'huge white stallion' that kept coming in from nowhere. Since then, it's reported, there have been many further sightings of the phantom white stallion.

There is a story to explain this phantom. When the Sackvilles were selling the property to the industrialist James Gwynne in 1896, a certain farmer was furious that his offer to purchase had been ignored and so he galloped on his white stallion to Michelham to confront the family. But he tumbled off his steed, and the horse galloped away without him, no doubt leaving him with an even redder face than he had in the first place.

John Leame – A Charming Gentleman

A gentleman often approached friends of the Wrights, who once owned the manor, at the gatehouse. The gentleman pointed in the direction of the house as though to direct people, but he always remained silent. He looked like an Augustinian prior, with a haircut styled to resemble Jesus' crown of thorns, a dark cloak and sandals. After the visitors turned around to thank their 'guide' they'd be amazed to find that he had disappeared.

In some reports, people believe the apparition to be that of John Leame, (sometimes spelt 'Leem') who was prior from 1374 to 1417 and who was responsible for the building of the gatehouse he frequents. He was a person greatly admired for his kindness and benevolence. John Leame had greatly loved Michelham Priory and he was a very popular prior. He'd also got the villagers together to defend the area against the French raiders.

Here are a number of strange incidents reported by David Scanlan:

- The shade of a melancholy woman in grey can be seen staring into Michelham Priory's moat. It's believed her family, the Childrens, were once tenants here, and one of their sons was killed when his clothes were caught and tangled in the watermill. The story is unconfirmed but there are child graves of the family in Arlington Churchyard. Another ghost reported is that of the Gray Lady, who tends to stay around the gatehouse and who also stands on the bridge gazing sadly into the moat. Sightings of the Gray Lady have been reported on many occasions. Someone suggested she may have been a young Sackville, who had drowned in the moat, while a version taken from *Ghosts of the South East* by Andrew Green claims the phantom woman's baby daughter had drowned. Whether these are separate ghosts or different versions of the same ghost, is a matter for speculation.

- Chris Tuckett, a property manager, once moved into the Priory. He met David Scanlan in 2004 and told him he'd heard furniture moving in the night. He got out of bed to investigate and, sure enough, a piece of furniture had changed position and one of its castors had scraped and marked the floorboards. Then, Chris discovered a figure-of-eight carved into the floor – a phenomenon that could only have occurred by the furniture repeatedly moving in the same way.
- One evening, Chris Tuckett returned to the Priory. He locked the door behind him, but on the way upstairs, he passed a man coming down. Recalling he'd locked the door, making it impossible for the man to exit the building, Chris rushed back downstairs to let him out. But there was no one in the building – and Chris had the only set of keys in his possession!

Other paranormal manifestations claimed to haunt the Priory are:

- The Elizabethan Lady who haunts the Tudor room.
- The Black Phantom, who descends a staircase – that's no longer there – so that he (or she) appears to float from ceiling to floor.
- Sometimes music can be heard playing on a phantom harpsichord.

In his book, *Ghosts of the South East*, Andrew Green includes the following bizarre paranormal activity:

- In 1972, a thin, tragic woman with a small dog glided past visitors as they were waiting for tickets, despite being warned that pets were not allowed. But the woman didn't stop to heed the warning. A woman who was waiting to pay, complained about the other woman for barging in ahead of them without a ticket – but then, to everyone's surprise, the figure faded away and vanished. It was suggested that she may have been the mother of a young Sackville woman who drowned. (Maybe this story is a different version of the Sackville drowning story as told by David Scanlan, but whatever the case, it seems the Sackvilles had an unfortunate relationship with water.)
- Also around the 1970s, a young couple saw the figure of a middle-aged, very handsome man in a cloak, descending from the ceiling. After he landed in front of the fireplace, he then glided away through a doorway. If that wasn't enough, a female ghost in a Tudor gown (described in some reports as the Lady in Blue)

suddenly appeared from the western end of the room, and also glided past the visitors in pursuit of the vanished man. Could there once have been a staircase where the fireplace now stands? asks Andrew Green.

We know it's common for ghosts to be sighted ascending stairs no longer there, or floating several feet above the ground – or who even appear to be walking on their knees. It means that when they were alive, stairs existed where they exist no longer, or the ground level was different, either higher or lower, than it is today. This probably also explains why ghosts so frequently walk through walls – because the wall probably wasn't there during their human lifetime on earth.

There are a few other odd stories indicating paranormal activity, for example, according to Andrew Green, bells have rung out when neither of the two Michelham bells were being activated. Debra Munn in *Sussex Haunted Heritage* suggests this might have been caused by the psychic echo of a bell sold by the Priory during the Dissolution of the Monasteries.

Other phenomena cited in *Sussex Haunted Heritage* include a window opened when there was no one there to push it; cold spots, orbs, stuff scattered on the floor or sent flying across the room; bedclothes and mattresses tossed onto the floor; strange smells; unexplained crashes and bangs; unexplained footsteps and horses' hooves that have startled visitors. Also, of course, several sightings of canons in black.

As a result, it's been subjected to a number of paranormal investigations that have produced startling findings. Several mediums independently came up with the name 'Rosemary' although no one really knows who Rosemary actually was. During filming of a television drama, after some wigs had been washed and left to dry overnight, they were discovered next day lying all over the floor. This happened despite the area being locked and alarmed.

One particularly scary incident related by Debra Munn involved a Hallowe'en paranormal investigation in 2004 carried out by the Children of the City and which concluded with a séance. The investigators claim a man called Thomas rudely told them to leave his house. When they didn't at first comply, he repeated his request several times. There was some dispute as to whether this was former owner Thomas Sackville, or possibly even Thomas Cromwell.

The name 'Michelham' means: 'the hamlet in the bend of the river', this being the Cuckmere, which drives the famous watermill.

David Scanlan's interest in the paranormal began after he witnessed poltergeist phenomena some years ago. As a result he established the Hampshire Ghost Club (www.hampshireghostclub.net) with the aim of getting people together to investigate ghosts and also the possibility of life after death.

CHAPTER 11
THEATRE AND GALLERY GHOSTS STILL SEEKING ATTENTION

Cases of haunting in theatres are generally well-documented and are often assigned to former actors and actresses who performed on their stages. These were characters who were larger than life during their physical lives – and they manage to remain larger than life in death by continually treading the illustrious boards that brought them fame and fortune. You can even see a video of one if you go onto You Tube – read on to find out how.

The Royal Hippodrome's You Tube Ghost

The Royal Hippodrome opened in 1883 as the New Theatre Royal and Opera House and was renamed the Hippodrome in 1904. Located in Seaside Road, the Hippodrome has a ghost you can easily watch on www.youtube.com simply by keying in the words: 'Ghost Royal Hippodrome Eastbourne'. You have to look very closely to spot the ghost, as the video pans the whole theatre, while the moving phantom image is small - but the ghost is unmistakeable and convincing. If you don't see it properly first time, replay the video. Maybe this is the ghost of a man first spotted during the 1990s, which would appear in the theatre and then suddenly vanish. The man is not alone either – some people also report sightings of a woman partial to taking her place in one of the seats in the Grand Circle. She chooses a different seat every time.

The Hippodrome's Special Little Girl

According to Tina Lakin's *Haunted Theatres of East Sussex* (The History Press, 2008) there is also a curly-haired little girl in old-fashioned dress of lace and frilly petticoats, aged around ten years, who is often spotted by actresses in their dressing rooms. However, this is a very prim and proper little girl ghost as she never appears in the male dressing rooms and is reported, always, to sit quietly watching the beautiful actresses preparing their make-up. The little girl was called Emily Fogarth in real life, and she was the daughter of a theatre manager appointed when the theatre first opened. Tragic Emily died of a weak heart at twelve years old after catching bronchitis.

The Royal Hippodrome

Heavy chains clang in the Hippodrome's interior

Specialising in performing in Victorian horror pictures, actor Tod Slaughter (19.03.1885 – 19.02.1956) is said to haunt the Hippodrome Theatre. His full name was Norman Carter Slaughter and his work was melodramatic and, by today's standards, rather over-the-top. His ghost, which often appears to take the form of a poltergeist, is similarly larger than life. It's said the many horror productions in which he was involved, including those featuring Jack the Ripper, the serial killer of Whitechapel, and Sweeney Todd, the Demon Barber of Fleet Street, have portrayed an evil that has been absorbed into the very walls of the Theatre.

The ghost of Tod Slaughter, (1885-1956) makes an awful lot of noise and the sound of heavy chains being dragged around are one of the most extreme manifestations of his presence. Sometimes Russ Conway's piano is heard playing and there are other inexplicable noises, like keys travelling through the Theatre, often at night when the building is plunged into ghostly darkness. Could these paranormal phenomena be anything to do with the male presence on the Youtube.com video?

Tod Slaughter was born in Newcastle-upon-Tyne and presented his very last macabre performance at The Royal Hippodrome Theatre. Eventually he died of coronary thrombosis. In an interview by Mr. Brian Lambert with Mr. Dave Davis in *The Paranormal Watch*, Volume 1, Issue 4, dated June 2009, 'Spirits Acting Up, the Eastbourne Hippodrome', Mr. Davis confirmed that most of the paranormal activity seems to be laid

Sweeney Todd liked to scare children. Tod Slaughter in the title role

at the door of Tod Slaughter. However, a tall gentleman is black has also been sighted all over the place, said Mr. Davis, for example, in the upper circle, the fly floor and the dress circle. He's thought to be an old manager although some people think he is Tod Slaughter himself. 'I doubt we will ever figure out who or what he is,' said Mr. Davis.

Mr. Davis told Brian Lambert about a painter working in the stalls who glanced up to the upper circle, only to see a gentleman in black staring down at him. When the painter went to investigate, he was amazed when the figure vanished in front of his eyes. Another manager, Mr. John Playdell, told Mr. Davis about an usherette, who encountered the tall, black-attired gentleman ghost, and was totally freaked out when he disappeared through a wall.

Other Hippodrome Phenomena

- Around two centuries ago, it's said a theatre manager cut himself on a kitchen knife and subsequently died from septicaemia, and that his ghost still haunts the theatre. Could it be that this is the man in the You Tube video and not Tod Slaughter?
- Other people have reported being touched and tugged.
- Some investigators have experienced an uneasy atmosphere, as though the ghosts are hostile and want to block them out.

The Devonshire Park Theatre – Orbs and a Violin

Strange orbs are said to move around the interior of this fine theatre, which dates from 1884. The colours vary from a deep blue fading to silvery white. According to

Haunted Theatres of East Sussex, some people says the orbs are the spirit of Annabella Charlestone, who died of a broken heart when she found her husband with another woman.

In the '60s through to the '70s, it's claimed that a phantom violinist occasionally put in an appearance although there have been no recent sightings.

The Haunted Art Gallery

The Towner Art Gallery at Gildredge Park in the Old Town dates from the 1770s and was owned by a Dr. Lushington who lived from 1734-1779 when it was a manor house. Its last incumbent, the Reverend Towner, bequeathed the house to the Council on his death. It opened as a gallery in 1923, although, much later in 2005, its artworks were being prepared for relocation to the Cultural Centre in Devonshire Park.

During the time the Towner Art Gallery resided at the manor, staff reported a strong smell of horses when they visited the spooky old cellars, which were now used for storage, although there have been no horses anywhere near the place for over one hundred years. Also, footsteps were heard overhead – and it was more than just one phantom as soft conversation could also be heard. Frustratingly, it wasn't quite loud

The old Manor House at the site of the Towner Art Gallery

enough to understand the ghostly gossip. A ghost was once sighted in the Long Gallery, and she's thought by some to be a former housekeeper.

The Tally Ho, whose talkative little girl ghost is described in Chapter 6 is located a short distance away from the old manor house, but on the opposite side of the road. There's also The Lamb close by, with its child ghosts. Seems the Old Town ghosts still have plenty to say for themselves!

CHAPTER 12

THE PHANTOM HEADLESS HORSE OF EASTBOURNE REDOUBT

It may seem strange that a phantom headless horse should haunt the site of the fortress known as the Eastbourne Redoubt. No one was ever killed at the Redoubt – and although it was bombed twice during the war, nobody was actually hurt by enemy action. According to staff, no one has even *died* there, except maybe of old age or a cold winter. This large, circular fortress was built between 1804 and 1810 to defend Eastbourne against invasion by Napoleon. It was also a barracks and supply depot for the neighbouring Martello Towers.

Now Eastbourne Redoubt, it is claimed, is haunted by the ghost of a terrified horse decapitated in the Charge of the Light Brigade in the 1850s, an appalling event of the Crimean War that was immortalised a few years later in the fine poem by Alfred Lord Tennyson. Around 113 men were slaughtered in this terrible battle, 134 were wounded, and our phantom horse was just one of five hundred horses sacrificed in a military action fought against overwhelming odds.

Into the Valley of Death Rode the Six Hundred

The Battle of Balaclava was fought on 25 October 1854 – mounted soldiers were forced to ride up a valley to capture Russian guns and were mercilessly gunned down on both flanks, knowing, as they pressed forward, that there was no hope of coming out of this hellhole alive. The soldiers were under orders from Lord Cardigan, who, according to Christopher Lee in *This Sceptred Isle,* subsequently returned to his yacht to bathe, dine, quaff champagne and then retire to his own nice warm bed.

There was a terrible irony to all of this. Lord Cardigan's commander, sixty-six-year-old Lord Raglan had not expressed his orders very clearly, resulting in the Light Brigade being mobilised to charge the *wrong* guns. In all, a heroic but tragic military blunder. Here is a stanza from Lord Alfred Tennyson's poem describing the terrible ordeal faced by both men and horses:

Cannon to right of them,
Cannon to left of them,
Cannon in front of them
Volley'd and thunder'd;
Storm'd at with shot and shell,
Boldly they rode and well,
Into the jaws of Death,
Into the mouth of Hell
Rode the six hundred.

The Light Brigade's Connection with Eastbourne Redoubt

The phantom horse's owner was a soldier of the Queen's Royal Irish Hussars, a regiment that saw tragic action at that famous battle. According to the poem, the men, on their horses, were subjected to inhuman terror, as they were 'forced into the Jaws of Death' and this is where the living version of the phantom horse lost its head.

The saddle that once belonged to Eastbourne Redoubt's headless phantom horse.
Photographed with permission

Poised to target
the French
invaders
– a cannon at
Eastbourne
Redoubt

The Queen's Royal Irish Hussars were formerly stationed at Eastbourne Redoubt and surely this must be the reason the horse has returned to haunt his former home, presumably a place where he once felt safe and secure. So now, unable to move on, the headless phantom horse wanders the hall in what is now the museum, where its former saddle is mounted on the wall in a window display (see image).

The Crimean War began in July 1835 when Russia occupied territories belonging to Turkey, Britain and France. Turkey was first to declare war on Russia over a disagreement about concessions. Florence Nightingale treated in a hospital near the Front lines and Mary Seacole tended them on the battlefield at her own expense.

It costs just £3 to visit the museum to see the display, including the wall-mounted saddle that once adorned the back of the headless horse. It's a fine collection and well worth a visit.

CHAPTER 13

PARANORMAL PEVENSEY

The village of Pevensey is located on a ridge of land five miles north-east of Eastbourne. This is where, in 1066, William the Conqueror arrived with his fleet and landed at Pevensey. Its focal point is Pevensey Castle which was originally built by the Romans to defend their empire in Britain. The Castle also helped to repel the threat from the Spanish Armada, from wily Napoleon and, in later times, from Hitler.

A Desperate Lady

It wasn't easy for highborn ladies in the fourteenth century, who were expected to multi-task in ways we cannot imagine. Lady Joan Pelham was left to defend Pevensey Castle during a terrifying seige by the army of Richard II. The difficulty was that her husband John was engaged in fighting against Henry Bolingbroke (later to become King Henry IV) Her pleas to John to return to help defend his wife and home from the enemy eventually persuaded him to comply. But – not before his unfortunate wife had been thoroughly traumatised by his absence and lack of protection.

The trauma was so great that it's said its residual energy has become trapped forever within her pale ghost, which still lingers along the upper castle walls at dusk. Her anxious eyes rake the horizon for the sight of her returning husband, hurrying to save her from King Richard's fierce soldiers. According to Richard Jones' *Haunted Castles of Britain and Ireland*, many people have reported sightings of Lady Joan Pelham's misty form hovering above the ramparts. A sighting was reported as recently as 1976, when some young men out on the razzle were badly freaked out by the apparition of the famous lady ghost.

A Royal Poisoner?

The second contender for the manifestation of the Grey Lady is also named Joan. This is Joan of Navarre, who was the second wife of King Henry IV. It's claimed Joan lost favour with Henry and things got pretty nasty. In 1419, Joan was accused by Friar Randolph of trying poison the King through witchcraft and the unfortunate woman was arrested and put into prison in Pevensey Castle. There she remained in custody until the King granted her pardon on his deathbed.

A *Wronged Stepmother*

The final contender for the Grey Lady haunting was a married woman, Duchess Joanna of Brittany, who set her sights on Henry IV. When her elderly husband died, she managed to get Henry to marry her by proxy, and a year later, in 1403, Joanna came to

Left: Pevensey Castle by Piotr Zarobkiewitz, with permission (Wikipedia)

Below: Part of Pevensey Castle's ramparts

England to be with her husband. A few years later, he too died, and was succeeded by his son, Henry V. It seems that greedy Henry wasn't too smitten by his stepmother and accused her of witchcraft so he could confiscate her property. To make matter worse, he incarcertated his stepmother for three years at the Castle – a horrible punishment – although later, as he lay dying, he felt guilty and recanted. Joanna was released but so traumatised that it's believed it is *her* ghost and not the shade of either of the two Joans, that drifts miserably around the grounds and walls of Pevensey Castle.

The Smallest, Spookiest Dungeon

On www.mystical.co.uk, the ghost expert Andrew Green describes a small dungeon or cellar within the Castle grounds, and accessed down a stone spiral staircase. The smells from this tiny den of horror are so repellent that dogs won't go near the entrance, and would certainly never venture below.

Strange Experiences for Dogwalkers

In her article, 'The Ghosts of Pevensey Castle' by Elizabeth Wright, a more recent paranormal encounter occurred early morning, three days in a row, by a dog-walker. The resident of Westham used to take his dog into the castle grounds and one day, spotted a figure in black across the meadow. Nothing unusual in that, and when it happened again the following day, he simply assumed it was another dogwalker. The third day, he picked up a stick to throw for his dog but, as he hurled it into the air, the wind propelled it towards the figure so that it landed behind it. The man's dog raced off in pursuit – and passed right through the 'spectre' of the man in black. The dogwalker beat a hasty retreat and although he returned the next day, he never saw the phantom in black again.

According to Eastbourne man Charlie Prangnell, he had a paranormal experience of a slightly different nature while walking his dog up to Pevensey Castle around midnight. Charlie is highly sensitive to spirit vibrations so when he heard a huge splashing in the moat, he decided not to investigate but instead took off home. But he did go again the following night. To his consternation, exactly the same thing happened; the splashing sounded scary and sinister in the darkness of the Castle grounds and Charlie left.

But unlike the previous man, Charlie was now far too freaked out to go there again.

Other phenomena mentioned by Elizabeth Wright in her article for www.timetravel-britain.com are as follows:

- Paranormal investigations had shown the dungeon and the North Tower were haunted by floating orbs and have a decidedly sinister feeling about them. Departed spirits or maybe beings from a parallel universe? No one knows for certain.
- The sighting of a marching Roman centurion and the ghost of a drummer boy beating loudly on his instrument to warn of a Saxon attack have been reported.

Pevensey Castle's impressive walls

Pevensey Castle was originally a Roman fort and was built in the third century to defend against Saxon raiders. These fierce warriors massacred a number of Britons in 491. William the Conqueror built a wooden castle inside the walls of the stone fort. The wood was replaced by stone sometime during the twelfth century.

A Very Special Contribution

In *Sussex Ghosts and Legends*, Tony Wales tells the story of an enormous stone at the western boundary of Pevensey. It was deposited there by an old lady. This was her personal contribution to the foundations of Pevensey Castle and she had the precious artefact nestled in her apron. At the spot where the Castle now stands, her apron strings broke and down went the stone, where it remained.

Revenge of the Jealous Lover at the Old Mint House

The well-known story of the Old Mint House in the High Street, which dates from the fourteenth century, must be the source of one of the goriest ghost stories ever told. The house is built on the site of the original eleventh century Norman mint, right opposite

The old Mint House, Pevensey, location of an horrific murder

the Castle. The story concerns a merchant from London named Thomas Dight who, in 1586, became the tenant of the Old Mint House and moved there with his beautiful mistress. In another account it's claimed he brought her to the Old Mint House for a 'hunting holiday'. Either way, the mistress was much younger than Thomas, who often had to travel to London on business, leaving mistress Eleanor Fitzjohn alone and bored.

One day, when Thomas Dight returned home, he found the passionate Eleanor – who hadn't been expecting him – *en flagrante* with her young fisherman lover. Dight didn't just get mad – he went absolutely ballistic.

Presumably the jealous merchant had some help from his loyal henchmen to achieve the atrocities he then committed. First, having commanded his servants to tie up the pair, he cut out the young woman's tongue with a sharp knife from the kitchen. Then both lovers were dragged into another room known as the minting chamber, surrounded by stone walls. In the corner there was a chimney, for dealing with the poisonous fumes. Here, a fire was built in the middle of the floor. The young fisherman was trussed up by his legs from chains fixed from the ceiling over the open fire. The dampness of the wood used for the fire produced a lot of smoke and prolonged his agony. His tormentors were forced to leave the room, because of the choking smoke. Eventually Eleanor's young lover died from suffocation and heat while his dying lover watched helplessly just a few feet away. His body, it's said, was taken out and tipped over the village bridge, to be carried out to sea.

There are different accounts about the mistress's end; in one, Dight had his wife taken upstairs still tied up, and she was left in that dark, dismal room to die of starvation and was buried nearby. In another version, she bled to death from the severance of her tongue. Thomas Dight, it is said, confessed to his terrible crime on his deathbed.

After such a terrible end, it's not surprising this lady cannot rest. Now a room in the Old Mint House is described as 'The Haunted Chamber' where, it's said, her spirit still lingers in torment. One brave man stayed there overnight, reportedly for a 'dare' and he claimed afterward to have seen her. He wrote a full account about her as appears on www.yeoldesussexpages.com

He had fallen asleep easily enough but was woken by an irregular tapping from around the window area. Looking up, he saw a face pressed against the exterior of the window and then, to his horror, 'something' came through the window and stood at the foot of the couch where he was lying. There was no question the window was closed to intruders, as it was already securely fastened when the man had retired.

The figure he described was that of a young woman in a dress with a tight-fitting bodice and sleeves, very full around the hips. It looked as though it came from Elizabethan times because she wore a small ruff around her neck and a lacy headdress. After a moment, she moved to the window and disappeared, and the terrified man leapt off the couch and dashed outside to find his friend. They came back to the room with him and when they checked the window; they saw that the fastening had not been interfered with. Since then, it's claimed her pale face has been seen gazing from the Mint House window on several occasions. One couple claimed seeing the face at the window in 2003 while drinking at The Royal Oak and Castle. Other reports claim that the woman is seen running around the Mint House screaming her head off, her mouth running with blood. Could this be the demented shade of the tormented Eleanor Fitzjohn? Yet other reports have said that hers is a silent ghost – yet they have the feeling she is always trying to say something.

The old Mint House has another sad story to tell as related by a barmaid of The Royal Oak and Castle – it is also haunted by the phantom of a woman who had thrown her baby downstairs, and sometimes the baby's screams can be heard.

The 600-year-old, half-timbered Mint House has also been used as an hotel but currently it is a very upmarket antique shop. There was a mint here back in 1076 AD, although The Mint House, as it now stands, was actually erected in 1342 AD. Its interior was later changed in the mid sixteenth century. Coins were originally minted here in the time of William the Conqueror and it's believed this continued until the reign of Henry II. According to some sources, there was once a subterranean passage which ran beneath the walls into the Castle.

The Poltergeist Next Door to the Post Office

Next door to the post office in Pevensey, was a little cottage, where Charlie Prangnell worked as a teenager in the late sixties, painting and decorating for the owners, the Butlers. While he was in a front bedroom with his dusting brush in his back pocket, it was suddenly ripped from his trousers and hurled to the floor. Charlie went to see his brother. 'Are you mucking about with me?' he asked belligerently. His brother denied culpability.

Then the housekeeper explained: 'There's a poltergeist coming out of the cupboard in that room,' she told Charlie. Charlie shivered. He'd had his back to the cupboard at the time.

Residual Hauntings – Armies on the Move

There are, allegedly, at least two phantom armies on the warpath in the Pevensey area. It's been reported that a phantom Roman army regularly marches on its way to the Castle. Alarmingly, there's also a ghostly Norman army led by William Rufus, later King William II. The Roman army's footsteps and voices can be heard although the soldiers cannot be seen, while the latter army, led by the cruel and tyrannical Red King (nicknamed for his complexion; it's said he actually had long, blond hair) can be clearly seen but not heard. However, there is a conflicting story about the Roman army – that they can be seen but only from the waist upwards because they are marching on the old road, which was lower than the present ground level. Also, to complicate matters further, there's said to be a regiment of Roundheads on the march, possibly on their way to see off a few Royalists.

Phenomena such as these are known as 'residual hauntings' because it's just like a video being played back of an historic event, with no interaction between eyewitness and ghosts. Some people think the apparitions are due to a trick of the light or even mass hysteria. Others say they are down to a rip in the space-time continuum – although for most of us that's a difficult concept. However, since all the phantom soldiers inhabited different time zones, whether visible or audio, they will probably never meet.

A Case of *déjà vu*

In his book *Country Ways in Sussex and Surrey*, Anthony Howard describes an experience told to him, that related to the old smithy in Peelings Lane, Pevensey. The smithy dates back to the 1800s. At the time of writing, Sam Fanaroff worked there in copper, silver, pewter and brass. Mr. Fanaroff described to Anthony Howard his amazement when he came to Pevensey from South Africa and first saw the Castle. He knew at once that he'd seen it before even though he had never heard of it. Some years later he was told by a spiritualist that, in the eleventh century, he had actually lived in Pevensey. He claims that, surprising though that was, he had carried inexplicable images of the place throughout his life. Suddenly, everything came together like a jigsaw puzzle. 'It means that I feel part of this place,' he concluded.

The old court house and museum

A *Pevensey Haunted House*

Tina who serves behind the bar of The Smugglers Inn tells some spooky stories about the forbidding old house, The Gables, which stands on the bend opposite the castle ruins. During The Second World War, she explains how wounded soldiers were taken care of in the house. Since then, people have reported hearing the phantom cries of the injured men. It's also claimed that some former occupants heard the sounds of a rope creaking – apparently a man had hanged himself from a beam immediately above the bed, although nothing is known for sure about who this was or the reason for this tragic suicide.

More *Ghosts Haunting the Pevensey Area*

Most of the following phenomena from Pevensey village were reported in the *Eastbourne Herald* on 25 October, 2007 during interviews with the landlady and landlord (respectively) of the The Smugglers Inn and The Royal Oak and Castle. These have been combined with additional details obtained from other works of reference, as specified.

The Gables was a makeshift hospital in the Second World War

- The clattering hooves of the cavalry passing along the High Street.
- Spirits of unfortunate Pevensey residents of ancient times still cry out as they are thrown, with their hands and feet tied together, into the river from Pevensey Bridge. These victims of early local justice were, most likely, so-called 'witches'.
- The ghosts of people slain in a Saxon massacre.
- Paranormal investigators have spent several nights in the Old Court House and Museum. They report temperature fluctuations and weird glowing lights.
- A couple of hundred years ago, a young woman was murdered in the Elizabethan house next to Pevensey's church of St. Mary the Virgin. A family moved there during the 'seventies and reported a sighting of a young girl dressed as a Victorian glide across the landing and through a wall at the end. This event happened each evening at precisely 11.00pm, according to her article 'The Ghosts of Pevensey Castle' by Elizabeth Wright. Subsequently, an exorcism laid the phantom to rest.
- The Vicar of the Church of St. Mary the Virgin in Westham was working late one night at the church, which was mostly in darkness. All its doors were secure and locked. He heard a loud hammering on the main big oak doors, which began to shake. As he put his hand on the door, the hammering stopped. The bold vicar opened the door and peered outside but there was nothing there. Some people think this was the ghost of a smuggler who wanted to reassure himself the Excise

men were safely in church, so the loot could be moved without hindrance from the law.

- Also seen in the churchyard of St. Mary, Westham, is a more modern ghost, described by Judy Middleton in her book *Ghosts of Sussex*. This ghost wears a run-of-the-mill grey suit and may be seen coming towards the church or leaving it. Judy Middleton quotes a Mr. Michael Stone, who saw the man in a grey in 1978. Mr. Stone said that he'd had a very good view of the phantom man and thought he was about 5'10" tall. Just as Mr. Stone smiled, greeted him with a 'Good afternoon' and went to open the gate, the phantom vanished from sight..
- People have seen a grey man in the churchyard of St. Mary the Virgin, carrying a walking stick. He walks along the path from the church door to the gate and then back again. One eyewitness described him as 'a dapper little gentleman,' who cheerfully bade them 'Good afternoon,' before disappearing.
- It is claimed the museum and prison cell in the village is haunted by the ghosts of those unfortunate people sentenced to death who must have quaked with fear as they awaited their fate. The prison still has spiked walls and stone benches and the original heavy oak doors. Sometimes people have actually *paid* to spend a night in the cell! It was once the smallest town hall in England.
- A local man reports having seen the phantom of a monk in his home and he assumed it was from the Priory.
- As for the provenance of some of these hauntings, it's said that Westham's Rattle Road is named after the hangman of Gallows Lane. The rattling heard is that of the bones of those who have been hanged. Also, going out of Pevensey towards Norman's Bay is Executioner's Bridge where the lives of those who'd upset the community were violently ended. Another source of the many tortured souls who haunt Pevensey?

CHAPTER 14

PHANTOM DRUMMING AND SOBBING AT HERSTMONCEUX CASTLE

Herstmonceux Castle, which is just eight miles north of Eastbourne, has its own grisly history as well as a few, mostly female ghosts and one extra-large, very masculine superghost. Between the porter's lodge towers is the Drummers' Hall and strange drumming has been heard coming from the area. Some reports claim that the drummer

Herstmonceux
Castle

sometimes leaves the hall and struts about the battlements. He is claimed to be nine feet high and a terrifying spectacle. According to local speculation, the drummer was a gardener who was co-operating with the Pevensey smugglers. With his tattoo, the enormous man sent signals to ensure the smugglers were aware when the 'coast was clear' and they could go about their business.

But there are two alternative stories to explain the phenomenon. In one account, a former owner, Lord Dacre, married a much younger and very beautiful wife, but he was actually a recluse and told his wife and servants to behave as though he were dead. In spite of this strange request, he became paranoid about all the dashing young fellows who gave her the eye. The insanely jealous old man took to beating hard on his drum to warn off any competitors for her favours. It seems she got fed up of his possessiveness and locked him up in a small cell, abandoning him there until he starved to death. Meantime, she went about her business of enjoying all her lovers with impunity.

But her cunning ploy rebounded on her as the drumming continued unabated after Lord Dacre's death, scaring off any prospective lovers. Eyewitnesses to the phantom drummer report that sparks fly off the drum as it is beaten with the metal drumstick. The third interpretation of this haunting is that the drummer is the phantom of a soldier who perished at the Battle of Agincourt with Henry V.

There is one other possible explanation, although it's not of a paranormal nature. Sceptics claim that the drummer was yet another invention of smugglers, this time to scare people away from the Castle, presumably because their loot was stashed somewhere in the vicinity. This, however, doesn't explain the repeated sightings, which continued long after the smugglers had disappeared into history.

Whoever the nine-foot drummer represents – whether a real drummer still devoted to his military duty, a Lord who even in death, is still obsessing about the loyalty of his lovely young wife, or a slaughtered soldier – he's clearly unaware that he is dead.

More Herstmonceux Ghosts

- Herstmonceux Castle has a ghost known as the White Lady. The White Lady is always terribly distressed. The story behind her appearances is that she was lured to the Castle by Sir Roger Fiennes, who fought with Henry V at the Battle of Agincourt and was responsible for building Herstmonceux Castle in 1441. Sir Roger Fiennes, it is claimed, forced himself upon the innocent young woman and eventually murdered her. Her shade is often to be seen close to the gatehouse or wandering listlessly around the moat.
- Then there are two animal ghosts. One is said to be the phantom ghost of Lord Dacre's own riderless steed, although other reports claim to have sighted Lord Dacre's ghost actually astride his horse. The other is a ghost donkey, with a young female phantom sitting astride him.
- Yet another female is known as The Grey Lady. This latter ghost may be that of a young girl who, in the eighteenth century, was imprisoned in the Castle until she starved to death, although it hasn't been possible to discover the nature of her alleged 'crime'. In certain parts of the Castle, her pitiful sobbing can be heard and her ghost has been seen drifting around the corridors.

How Herstmonceux Castle got its Name

Idonea de Herste married a nobleman called Ingelram de Monceux around the close of the twelfth century. The original 'manor' which pre-dated the Castle, was named Herste de Monceux, then Herste of the Monceux and finally Herstmonceux. The Castle was plundered to provide building materials in 1777, but was restored to its original glory in the early twentieth century. Edward I stayed at the Castle in 1302.

CHAPTER 15

THE CRUMBLES' GIRL GHOSTS

The ghosts of two young women, brutally murdered within four years of one another in The Crumbles, are said to haunt the area. The Crumbles is to the East of Easbourne and was once a barren place. No doubt the phantom women are still bewildered at the manner of their sudden and unexpected deaths and so are unable to rest in peace. The first account, that of the ghost of Irene Munro, has been substantiated by an incredible eye-witness report by Mr. Mike Hawkins, who lives in a new housing development on

Boats moored on the beach on the famous shingles in The Crumbles' area

Sovereign Harbour north in a ten-year-old house. Sovereign Harbour is actually built on The Crumbles.

Mike says, 'The moment I saw her black and white picture, I recognised her.' What's surprising is that the coastguard cottages where Emily Kaye, (the subject of the second account) was murdered, is located at the end of Mike's back garden, a fact substantiated by an old map. 'I did my homework,' he says, 'I checked and checked again. I spoke about it to family and again to a friend of the family and he said it had been seen before.' Mike is absolutely certain that what he saw on that terrifying day was the ghost of Irene Munro. A full account of his experience follows this account of the horrific murder of Irene Munro.

Irene Munro – a Macabre Holiday Romance

Irene Munro was murdered on 19 August 1920. A seventeen-year-old typist from London, she'd come to Eastbourne for her holiday and had taken lodgings not far from The Crumbles, between Eastbourne and Pevensey. The name 'The Crumbles' is derived from an Eastbourne beach.

In the middle of that Thursday afternoon, Irene Munro left her lodgings and went for a walk. She was a pretty girl with dark hair but looked older than her years, and soon she caught the eye of two men, Jack Aldred Field and William Thomas Gray. Both men were in their twenties and were ex-servicemen. William Gray was a married man. The three of them walked in the direction of The Crumbles, near the coast. But Irene Munro didn't return to her lodgings.

At first her landlady thought she'd probably gone to visit relatives in Brighton, but after a couple of days, on the Saturday, she started to worry and reported her missing. But by then, her dead body had already been found, hurriedly buried in the shingle. Irene had been discovered the previous Friday afternoon by William Weller, a thirteen year old lad who was picnicking on The Crumbles with his mum. William had run into a dip in the shingle and tripped on a human foot and so the horrible crime was revealed. The young woman's corpse was severely injured around the head and her face was disfigured, but she was easily identified by her distinctive green velour coat. After the police arrived on the scene, a heavy stone covered in blood was found nearby.

The two men might have got away with it as The Crumbles was a lonely place, but several witnesses claimed to have seen the three; Irene was a vibrant girl who would have attracted plenty of attention, including from some men working on the railway line. They said she seemed happy. After a description was compiled of the guilty men, they were recognised as locals and as unemployed men with bad reputations who were always chasing women for casual flings. They were charged with Irene's murder and their trial began at Lewes Assizes on 13 December that year, lasting five days. They pleaded not guilty. William Gray tried to arrange a false alibi with the assistance of other prisoners, but he was found out. Each man accused the other of the murder.

It was claimed in court that Irene Munro had a liking for older men and liked to flirt with them, but she had not been raped, so it was presumed that she had refused their sexual advances. Enraged, the two men had set about the young girl and killed her by crushing her skull with the rock. The men were convicted jointly of her wilful murder because they were acting together. They were hanged at Wandsworth Prison on 4 February, 1921. Now, unsurprisingly, the young girl has been unable to move on and her tragic ghost has been sighted around the area of The Crumbles where she met her death, including this most recent eyewitness account.

Mike Hawkins' Terrifying Encounter

Mike lives in the most cornerly house on the Harbour and The Crumbles was located to the left of his home. Four years ago, around midday, Mike was in the front room, while his wife was at her computer in their conservatory. Mike heard what he thought were screams outside, so he rushed out to the conservatory to ask his wife if she'd heard them too. She was already on her feet, asking the same question.

Mike opened the back door and looked out, remarking it was probably only foxes. However, the couple's black labrador was going ballistic and then, a loud scream pierced the air. It was clearly a female in distress.

'At this point my wife and I raced out of our front door and I climbed on a chair to look over the fence,' explains Mike. He'd grabbed a high powered torch as he left the house and his wife, who was six months pregnant at the time, passed it up to him. 'I shone the torch in the direction of the screaming – a woman in much distress was clambering towards me. She was only around twenty-five yards away. She was crying and it shocked me. Then I heard a male voice telling her to shut up, in a violent way, and another male voice telling the first to keep calm.' Mike couldn't see either of these male presences, only the distraught woman. Telling his wife to phone the police, Mike reassured the woman that help was on its way, then he and his wife went back inside. His wife locked the front door and Mike, taking the dog and a torch, ran for the back gate. The time it took him was no more than twenty seconds.

'At first, the dog was unusually scared and had to be dragged out. But when I got outside there was nothing – no sound – nobody!' Mike points out that it would have taken a fast walk of at least two minutes to get out of sight if the woman had been a living human.

With the frightened dog, Mike scoured the area around where the woman had been. Police, in four cars, also arrived and began searching the area, but found nothing. 'What haunted me,' says Mike, 'is that she looked straight at me. I'll never forget her pleas for help. She was unfazed at looking into my bright light.'

It wasn't only Mike who'd heard the dreadful screams. A neighbour also heard them and was unable to sleep that night. This neighbour even went out at 6am next morning to search for the body and expecting to find it, but to no avail.

'Although the police found nothing, I later researched some history after someone told me about The Crumbles murders. What I read shook the life out of me – *I believe I saw a ghost*,' says Mike. The black and white photo he later found during his research convinced him that this was definitely Irene Munro. 'I assumed, at the time, that the girl was drunk and on her way home from the pub or something. It was only when I saw her over my fence that I thought differently. I'm open-minded and I know what I saw, along with my wife and a neighbour.'

Emily Kaye – said to Haunt the Site of her Murder

A book review dated 20 August 2007 in the *Mail Online* (www.dailymail.co.uk) cites the case of Emily Kaye who was murdered in 1924 at The Crumbles. Police had chanced upon a gruesome discovery, a number of decomposed and decomposing human body parts. The crime became known as The Bungalow Murder.

These human remains turned out to belong to recently murdered Emily Kaye, who'd had a married lover, fraudster and embezzler, Patrick Herbert Mahon. Patrick Mahon had also been convicted of robbery with violence, but nevertheless was said to have had 'winning ways'. Successful rogues are, of course, always believable! Through his wife, Mavourneen's influence, Mahon had been appointed sales manager of a company in Sunbury where he met typist Emily Beilby Kaye, who was thirty-seven years old and worked for an accountancy firm. He and Emily set up a love-nest, a bungalow at The Crumbles. She wanted him to leave his wife for her.

The couple argued in their 'love-nest' over a proposed trip to South Africa. There was another complication; Patrick Mahon had also taken up with a young woman from Richmond called Ethel Duncan. On on 12 April, 1924, it's alleged Mahon bought a saw and a knife before he travelled to Eastbourne to meet with his lover. His wife believed he had gone on a business trip. Emily, who was crazy about Mahon, had already told her friends she was engaged to be married to him and about her plans for them to visit South Africa. But he hadn't bothered to sort out his passport, which caused a quarrel between them.

According to Patrick Mahon, during the argument, Emily attacked him and then fell and hit her head against a coal bucket, and as a result, she died. Her lover cut her body into pieces with a butcher's saw, then, in a vain attempt to hide the evidence, he burned and boiled body parts and then threw limbs and organs out of a train window. Then he went off to London to meet Ethel and bought her dinner, inviting her to join him at the bungalow the following Easter weekend. Ethel suspected nothing.

Later, Mahon's wife, who was, understandably suspicious as he'd been away from her for two weekends, searched his pockets and discovered a cloakroom ticket for Waterloo Station. A Gladstone bag in the locker contained some bloodstained clothing. A police officer waited to intercept Mahon when he arrived to collect the Gladstone bag. His excuse, that the blood came from dog-meat he had purchased, didn't work – the bloodstains were, in fact, found to be human. Sir Bernard Spilsbury, who examined the body of Emily Kaye, found that she was pregnant. Her head, however, was missing.

Right to the end, Mahon insisted Emily had died accidentally. In his book, *Sussex Tales of Mystery and Murder* author W. H. Johnson quotes Mahon: 'We quarrelled over certain things and in a violent temper she threw an axe at me. It was a coal axe. It hit me a glancing blow. Then I saw red. We fought and struggled. She was a very big, strong girl. She appeared to be quite mad with anger and rage.' Mahon went on to describe how a chair was overturned and Emily's head was struck on an iron coal scuttle. He claimed to have tried to revive her but when this failed, he hid the body in a spare room under a coat. Then, next day he travelled to London and purchased a saw and, of all days, on Good Friday, this monster dissected his lover's body. (The precise details are too horrible to repeat.) Another distressing aspect of this case was that she was several weeks pregnant when she was murdered.

It was also found that Patrick Mahon had been appropriating Emily Kaye's savings for himself, a fact that further incriminated him. What's more, Mahon had previous 'form'. His criminal record included being fired for forging a cheque in his native Liverpool and he was once imprisoned for five years after a maid had caught him breaking into a bank. He'd hit her with a hammer! In spite of all this, his wife, Mavourneen, had stuck by him. (In some reports the wife is called *Mavourneen*, in other she is *Jessie*. Possibly 'Jessie' was a nickname.)

The judge described the murder as the 'most cruel , repulsive and carefully-planned murder' and like the murderers of Irene Munro, Mahon was tried at Lewes and hanged at Wandsworth Prison. The execution took place on 2 September, 1924.

Unsurprisingly, after such a terrible end to her physical life, it seems likely that Emily Kaye's spirit is unable to rest in peace, although I regret, in spite of my best efforts, I could find no fully-detailed eyewitness account, nor any properly documented article or book references to sightings of her ghost. People have talked to me about it albeit rather vaguely, and there are a few references on websites about how, very soon after her death, Emily's mournful ghost was sighted lingering around the site of her murder, and one can imagine it looking pale and pathetic as it floated over the shingles. But all the sightings centre around the site of her murder and there seem to have been no reports whatsoever of ghostly manifestations around the area of the cottage where she stayed, originally located near Mike Hawkins' garden.

When The Crumbles was redeveloped, its original bank of shingle was useful to provide ballast, to the London Brighton and South Coast Railway in the 1860s. The access railway, called The Crumbles Tramway, closed down in the 1960s. The book reviewed, which featured Bernard Spilsbury, was called *Lethal Witness*, by Andrew Rose, published by Sutton Publishing.

The couple's love-nest bungalow was, for a while, a major tourist attraction and ghoulish entrepreneurs charged coachloads of visitors a shilling for a guided tour. Thankfully the bungalow was demolished in 1953 (or, in some accounts, 1954).

CHAPTER 16

TERRORS AT SEAFORD – THE TWYN HOUSE AND CORSICA HALL

The Cinque Port town of Seaford, just to the west of Eastbourne, has its own spooky stories. One of these centres round the area once occupied by the Parish Workhouse, which closed after the Poor Law Amendment Act of 1834.

The Workhouse site was formerly the location of a medieval hospital. There are conflicting reports as to whether this was the Hospital of St. John's, a leper hospital, or the Hospital of St. James of Sutton by Seaford. There are no apparent physical remains of either of the two medieval hospitals that once stood in Seaford, although it is reported that the sea destroyed the Hospital of St. John's in the fourteenth century. After the demise of the Workhouse, the Mayor lived in Twyn House while his assistant took up residence in Twyn Cottage, at 3-5 Blatchington Road.

According to the website www.gbhw.co.uk, the area is alive with paranormal activity. The gbhw team should know, since they were invited by a relative of one of their members to carry out an investigation into the weird occurrences that Twyn House is famous for. Mick Bony and the other members have granted permission for me to relate their discoveries when they visited the seriously-spooked residents of Twyn House.

They arrived on a Saturday evening quite recently and were welcomed by the owners, Wayne and Charlotte, and their son Jesse. The family were bursting with stories of their experiences. These are some of the incidents:

- Dark shadows have been reported, which stand over members of the family and watch them closely.
- Jesse, the son of the owners, said a large figure appeared in his bedroom. This terrifying figure compelled him to move out and into another room.
- There are unexplained knocks and bangs.
- Ornaments are 'jettisoned across the room and smashed on the floor'.
- Jesse's mum, Charlotte has seen shadows moving along the corridor. These disappear through the wall, as though on their way to what was formerly the old courtyard and leprosy hospital.
- The distinct shadowy outline of someone hanging from the old wooden beams in the main bedroom has been seen on several occasions.
- There is a smell of wax in the main bedroom, especially when the hanged figure, just mentioned, is sighted. There is nothing in the room to account for this smell.
- The family have a puppy which desperately resists being pushed or dragged into the main bedroom.
- The older dog refuses to enter the bar area, however much he is coaxed. Once the family tried to push him towards the doorway, but he was having none of it!

After so many hair-raising accounts, the members of the gbhw team were naturally determined to protect themselves while they were inside Twyn House and garden. They decided to get base readings and explore the general layout; including the ground and two upper floors. They found most activity centred in the main bedroom on the top floor and in the bar area on the ground level. The group set up their night-vision cameras and were able to take images of shooting orbs and strange lighting anomalies in the rooms, most of which proved especially active when they called upon the spirits that might be present. The team split themselves into groups, each group taking a room, alternating with one another throughout the night. They also held séances using an ouija board. At first nothing happened. But after about ten minutes, the activity began:

The Spirits make Themselves Known

At one séance, the glass started to move and a little boy of six came through and later other spirits made themselves available. Most of the spirits were good, but there were two that appeared to be bad spirits, one of which masked itself as something else, deliberately to mislead the investigators.

The Spirits Reveal their Physical Lives

The final séance brought forth some amazing results, believed to be as a result of the ouija board which increased the paranormal activity in the house. They discovered that the little boy was being taken care of by a soldier from the seventeenth century. Then

People have been holding séances for many years.
They became popular in Victorian times.

there was the nineteenth century master of the house who was still suffering pangs of guilt for having an extra-marital affair with a maid who became pregnant. When his wife discovered his infidelity, she hounded the young woman until she was driven to hanging herself from a beam in the main bedroom.

The other bad spirit revealed to the investigators that he had been a monk and that he had murdered others while living in the house in his physical life.

Feely-touchy Ghosts

The group recorded that the main bedroom was the coldest room, and the temperature within would rise and fall for no apparent reason, as proved by their digital temperature guage. But they could also physically feel the extreme changes. Once, when they asked the spirits to make a noise or touch one of them, they heard a tap from the area of the door. Then it happened two or three times more. Two members, Marlene and Jean were touched, respectively, on the top of the leg and the ankle. Again, there were orbs and lights moving around the room and recorded on the night-vision and digital cameras. At another vigil, Twyn House's co-owner, Wayne, had his leg touched and so he decided not to stay a moment longer, although the others remained to observe the shooting orbs and strange lights.

Watched in the Bar

Three members, Sandra, Gill and Marlow kept vigil in the bar, which was so cold it sent chills down their spines. The first thing was a loud thud – and the ubiquitous bright orbs and lights. All were convinced there was something watching them and felt increasingly uneasy.

The Cloaked Bar-ghost

After a further experiement using the ouija board, three members of the team ventured back into the bar, where they called out for responses. Two people, co-owner Charlotte and gbhw team member Jean, saw a dark form standing behind the bar. It was tall, and its upper part looked as though it was cloaked. Although their co-member Mick panned the night vision camera to the area, nothing was revealed. All the same, all three were sure there was something standing there and watching them, so they left the bar.

But they weren't the only ones leaving the bar. As he stepped through the doorway, Mick, who was the last to leave, felt cobwebs in his hair. Putting up his hand to grab at them, he asked Jean to help. She told him there was nothing there. But he could feel the coil of cobweb in his hand. 'I don't have much hair,' he says, 'it's cropped short, crew-cut style, so it wasn't my own hair I had in my hand.' He says he wasn't scared, more surprised, simply because he had always believed a ghost would never touch a living person.

Playing with a Ghost Child

A further experiment was conducted in the main bedroom by the three women. Believing the room contained the spirit of a child, they set up a 'trigger object' of two small plastic balls on a sprinkling of flour. Then they invited the spirit to play with the balls. There was an instant response; an orb shot towards the balls. Fortunately, this time they managed to capture the occurrence on the night-vision camera.

The Pressure of a Ghostly Presence

At another session in the main bedroom, with most of the members of the team present, Daniel, who was sitting on the bed, complained of a pressure on his stomach. It was most uncomfortable and he began sweating. He had to leave the room. One of the other members who remained in the room asked if it was the hanged woman who was trying to communicate through Daniel – and an orb was caught on the camera, leaving the end of the bed. There was also a wax-like smell present, reminiscent of candle-making, or maybe the smell from an old army uniform. Possibly this could have indicated the presence of the phantom soldier who took care of the little boy ghost.

You can read more ghostly stories on the website: www.gbhw.co.uk The acronym gbhw stands for Great Britain's Haunted Westcountry, although the group are interested in the paranormal anywhere in the country.

EVP – a Tool for Paranormal Investigators

EVP stands for Electronic Voice Phenomenon. This is what we know more familiarly as 'static' or 'background noise', an electronically generated noise that appears to resemble speech. Many people believe the unexplained sounds they hear on radios are of paranormal origin and investigators have been exploring ways of communicating with the spirits through tape recorders and other electronic devices since around the 1970s/1980s.

Corsica Hall – a House with a Complicated History

Built in 1740 by a merchant, John Whitfield, Corsica Hall was haunted by a tragic boy ghost. He was the son of Lord Francis Napier and was being tutored by a chaplain in May 1744 (in another account 1772) when the accident happened. The nine-year-old boy spotted a pistol left in the study and jokingly pointed it at his teacher, Mr. Loudon. 'Shall I shoot you?' he asked, mischievously. Thinking the gun wasn't loaded, the chaplain foolishly encouraged the little boy to shoot him, so the boy pulled the trigger and Mr. Loudon fell down dead.

Lord Napier died the following year but after that no tenant could be found because the house was, supposedly, haunted by the chaplain's ghost. Then merchant, Thomas Harben, bought the property. All this happened at Wellington near Lewes, but the house was subsequently moved, brick-by-brick, to its new location in Seaford by Thomas Harben. Although the house was later demolished and rebuilt, the ghost of the little boy persisted in haunting the site. According to a report in *The Sunday Express* by Kevin Gordon dated 17 April, 2009, he spooked the students attending the house on a training course – at this time it had become a college.

Corsica Hall was built on the site of an old mill and later it was renamed The Lodge by John Fitzgerald, a politican. It then became a convalescent home. An account of Corsica Hall's history and ghost appears in *Paranormal Brighton & Hove*.

CHAPTER 17

THE LOST SOUL AT CAVENDISH LODGE

Tradesmen, working at Cavendish Lodge in Cavendish Place, were the first recorded witnesses to a lost but friendly ghost, desperately searching for his proper place in the afterlife. They became so familiar with the confused spirit that they named him 'Charlie' and always called out 'Goodbye Charlie' when they left the property. The *Evening Argus* dated 30 January 1980 published an article entitled 'Ghostly Charlie', by Bob Wells, that detailed the many sightings of Charlie.

Cavendish Lodge was formerly a small hospital home for elderly gentlemen. At the time of the *Argus* report, it had been turned into holiday flats and was owned by Les and Irene Pearce who purchased it in October 1977. It was they who affectionately coined the nickname, 'Charlie'.

The first appearances, witnessed by the workmen, occurred in 1977, after Cavendish Lodge had been empty for a number of years. Wally Smith and Stan Gosden were builders and when they worked in the house; both spotted the dark shadowy figure – at first, independently. They didn't speak of their experiences to each other, each no doubt thinking he would not be believed by the other. Until one day, when they were together by the front door, and they shared a spooky experience. 'We saw a dark figure along the corridor,' said Stan. 'We went different ways to try to head him off, but we only met each other. There was nowhere he could have gone.'

This strange encounter set the men talking and they were relieved to discover each of them had seen the figure before, quite a few times. These independent sightings confirmed what they already suspected – that there really was a ghost on the premises. 'It was a bit frightening at first,' said Stan, 'but we got used to it.' The men experienced other paranormal occurrences, for example, once a door slowly opened and closed. It couldn't have been the wind because the door had a strong return spring.

Later, other tradesmen had similar stories to tell, including an electrician and a central heating engineer. Co-owner, Mr. Les Pearce, took up the story. 'I was about as sceptical a person as you could meet,' he said. 'I gave those blokes a real ribbing when they told us what they had seen. But then it happened to me.' At the time of the sighting, Les Pearce was with a friend and both saw a movement downstairs. Alarmed, Mr. Pearce seized a piece of wood to use as a club. Meanwhile, the friend hurried around the side of the house to head the figure off. Mr. Pearce hurried downstairs. 'When I got down there, I could find nothing. I bashed about with the club because I felt a bit scared,' he said.

The fine building formerly known as Cavendish Lodge in Cavendish Place.

Mr. Pearce insisted that if he felt the ghost had an evil influence, he wouldn't hesitate to call in an exorcist, but he was positive it was a friendly presence. He explained how one day he was talking to his wife, Irene, when he saw someone pass by a fire door. 'I hurried out, but he had gone. It looked like quite a short man with some sort of black cowl over his head,' he explained.

Where did Charlie come From?

It's always fascinating to try to work out the possible source of any paranormal sighting, although such theories will always contain an element of informed guesswork. Mr. Pearce favoured the theory that since the apparition began to appear at a time when the United Reformed Church in Old Pevensey Road was being demolished, this might have disturbed Charlie. As the church was located right opposite Cavendish Lodge, Charlie may simply have glided across the road in his search for a new home to haunt. The Sussex exorcist, Mr. John Junor, also confirmed it was possible that the apparition had been roused by the demolition of the lovely old church. 'This sounds very much like a lost soul that has yet to find its proper place. A spirit can be disturbed by such things as demolition, new people arriving in a house, or even furniture being moved. I would think that the spirit will appear again at some stage,' said John Junor.

Cavendish Lodge was around the same age as the The United Reformed Church, which was founded in 1862 and closed in 1973. Its last minister, the Revd T. John Williams, had died in October 1978.

CHAPTER 18

A GHOST WITH RED HAIR AND AN ANGEL

Tristan Morell who practises as a clairvoyant and spiritualist at Eastbourne's Enterprise Centre, says he is in contact with spirits everyday – because his clients bring them along, even if they don't realise it. Tristan explained that although his spirit connections are numerous, most are also confidential and, out of loyalty to clients, he was only able to talk about two of them. 'For someone who is psychic, the spirits are everywhere,' says Tristan.

At this point it might be helpful to define the differences between three terms for paranormal communication, psychic, medium and clairvoyance, as there seems to be considerable confusion and some overlap, even in dictionary definitions. Here are some precise definitions as set out by Sharon@mystic-mouse.co.uk:

Psychic – pertaining to mental forces, telepathy, extra sensory perception
Medium – contacting and being able to communicate with spirits of the dead
Clairvoyance - the ability to see things beyond our normal senses.

The Ghost with Red Hair

Once a Roman Catholic client came to Tristan for a reading, and he told her that a young girl with long red hair was standing beside her. She confirmed she had recently lost her daughter to leukaemia – and due to the treatment, her daughter had lost all her hair. The woman was overjoyed to hear that, in spirit, her daughter still had her beautiful hair. 'You've given me back my faith,' she told Tristan. 'But that's not really what I was trying to do,' explains Tristan. 'I never tell anyone what to believe or try to give my faith to them.'

Tristan's Angel

'My angel came to me years ago when I was living in a grotty bedsit,' says Tristan. The angel told Tristan he should broaden his horizons, and so he bought himself some Tarot cards and soon opened his colourful caravan in The Enterprise Centre. 'The angel told me that I was going to be successful and that I was going to teach – and now I have twenty-one students.'

At the time Tristan was also rather hard-up but his angel told him not to worry about money. 'The next day a letter in a brown envelope arrived for my partner and we found he had been awarded tax credits for £5,000,' says Tristan.

Tristan has also experienced instances of communicating and comforting distraught people shortly after their death, only to find out the actual details of their death sometime later. Again, he was unable to give any detailed accounts due to respect for his clients' privacy. His place of work can be found on the upper floor of The Enterprise Centre.

CHAPTER 19

AN EASTBOURNE NURSE RETURNS FROM THE DEAD

'One study found that 8 to 12 percent of 344 patients resusciated after suffering cardiac arrest had NDEs (near-death experiences) and about 18% remembered some part of what happened when they were clinically dead.' From the *Lancet*, 15 December, 2001.

Many people believe that NDEs are the hallucinations of a traumatised brain and that this is an entirely natural and predictable process. Yet those who have experienced this strange paranormal phenomenon find themselves entirely convinced that what has happened to them is far from a delusion, but a concrete reality that changes their lives for the better. Common changes are a much reduced fear of death combined with a feeling of being someone of special importance who has been favoured by God or by destiny. Central to all this is a belief in a continued existence after death.

Jeanette Atkinson, an Eastbourne student nurse, told of her near-death experience in 1979, when she was just eighteen years old. She says that, as a result, she no longer has any fear of death. Her story, by Danny Penman, appears on the website www. newsmonster.co.uk The young woman suffered a blood clot in her leg, causing the main vessels to her lungs to clog and deprive her body of oxygen. The medical prognosis was gloomy – Jeanette was not expected to survive. Here is Jeanette's experience, in her own words:

'The first thing I noticed was that the world changed. The light became softer but clearer. Suddenly, there was no pain. All I could see was my body from the chest downwards, and I noticed that the time was 9.00 pm. In an instant I found myself looking at the ceiling. It was only a few inches away. I remember thinking it was about time they cleaned the dust from the striplights.'

Photographic illustration of a near-death experience by Jesse Krauß, 29.10.2006

Jeanette's ethereal energy was pulled towards a bright light that appeared from a long tunnel. She describes how it seemed to be shaped like a corkscrew and how everything appeared 'fuzzy'. 'All I wanted to do was reach the beautiful lights at the bottom,' she says. The desire to pursue the lights was almost irresistible, but suddenly a loud voice commanded her to return. 'Come on, you silly old cow, it's not your time yet.'

When she returned to her body, Jeanette noted the time; she'd been out of her body for twenty minutes. She regained consciousness a few days later but still felt desperately ill. It was only some time later that she identified the voice she'd heard. It was her grandmother, who'd died when Jeanette was only three years old.

'I don't want to die again in the near future because I still have much to do,' says Jeanette. 'People see the pain and suffering of dying and equate that with death – but they're not the same. Death is the progression of life.'

What happens when people have NDEs?

In his book, *Transformed by the Light,* Dr. Melvin Morse (with Paul Perry) insists that near death experience is unlike any medically described hallucinations, nor does it resemble drug-induced hallucinations, schizophrenia, transient psychosis, psychotic breaks, anaesthetic reactions or dreams. Dr. Melrose says: 'The near-death experience is a logical and orderly event that involves floating out of the body, entering into darkness and experiencing a wonderful and indescribable light. Unlike people who have hallucinations or episodes of mental illness, NDEers have a feeling of being in control of the situation and do not feel detached from their being.'

Although the near-death experience varies from person to person, there are certain factors that seem to occur in a majority of cases. It's common for people experiencing an NDE to lose their fear of death and to feel an increasing need to help and value themselves and others. Some shared features for many people, including Jeanette, are hearing yourself pronounced dead, leaving your body with a great sense of peacefulness and moving through a dark tunnel towards a bright, welcoming light. Some people also report meeting with deceased friends and relatives.

Apart from NDE (life after death) some people also experience Pre-Birth Experience, (life before life). Reincarnation is an ancient, multi-cultural belief and there have been a number of amazing accounts of people who remember a past life – known as pre-birth experience. In some cases the memory dates prior to conception and sometimes between conception aned birth.

It hasn't been possible at the present time to find any examples of pre-birth experience in Eastbourne (although there may be such cases in the area, of course) but for those who are interested, there's a compelling story concerning a six-year-old American boy, James Leininger, who recalled being a Navy pilot in the Second World War. James suffered nightmares as he relived his experience of being shot down over the Pacific by the Japanese. He remembered his former life in specific detail and his account was thoroughly checked against the facts. This resulted in a book by his parents, Bruce and Andrea Leininger, with Ken Gross, *Soul Survivor,* available from Amazon.

CHAPTER 20

BEACHY HEAD'S SINISTER SPIRIT LEGACY

There are many ghost stories associated with the notorious suicide spot, Beachy Head, which is unsurprising considering the murderous and downright criminal activities that went on here in past times. It's claimed that, in medieval times, Beachy Head was one of the favourite places for the witches responsible for the rituals of deterring French invaders (presumably these were good, white witches) and that the notorious Aleister Crowley held demonic rituals at The Devil's Chimney. The Devil's Chimney was one of several chalk pillars which were split away from the cliff. The others were known as The Charleys. All eventually eroded and had disappeared into the sea by the early 1900s. It's said Aleister Crowley was photographed on The Devil's Chimney in 1894

Beachy Head and
the Lighthouse

and that on one of his climbs, he had to be rescued by the coastguard. Many people report feelings of sadness and hopelessness when in the vicinity.

Beachy Head's Smuggling Activities

Much of the coastline here was rife with smuggling, but people were poor and needy, with hungry children to feed. The Birling Gap provided a route for smugglers, who enticed vessels by setting up false lights in order to confuse and wreck ships in bad weather, and then plunder the goods for their own profit. Sometimes, according to http://www.riverocean.org.uk, a lantern would be tied to grazing animals, so that the movements were spotted out at sea and would even mimic the lights from another ship.

Capture by the authorities meant terrible punishments for the perpetrators but it merely points to the desperation of the unfortunate wretches responsible, who, no doubt, had families to feed and rent to pay. So it seems, both the persecutors and their victims were equally slaves to circumstance – and no doubt some of the ghosts who haunt the clifftops might well have been smugglers or sailors in their physical lifetimes, or possibly their abandoned wives or lovers.

Parson Jonathan Darby, became curator of St. Michael's Church in Litlington in 1692 was also the parson for East Dean and Friston, and responsible for burials of corpses from the wrecks. He was a compassionate man and wanted to do something to help. He decided on a fixed light and so excavated 'Parson Darby's Hole' in the caves already in existence, near to the Belle Tout Lighthouse. At the top of his 'chimney' he would set lights, and stand guard in the cave. It's claimed he saved many lives, even pulling individuals into the safe haven of the Parson Darby's Hole. Parson Darby died in 1726 allegedly of pneumonia, and is buried in Friston Churchyard.

Paradoxically, in Chapter 6, under the entry for The Tiger Inn, there is a reference to Parson Darby being implicated in Beachy Head's smuggling operations, a not-unusual activity for the clergy of that time. But again, people were poor and desperate and had hungry families to feed. The parson's cave is said to have been used by smugglers as late as the eighteenth century.

The highest point at Beachy Head is said to be around 535 feet above sea level. According to the Brighton *Evening Argus* of 4 March, 1980, the first recorded death leap was made by James Wyker who hurtled down the cliff in 1600.

Child Ghosts in the Moonlight

At the top of the cliffs, where they tower over the Birling Gap, are two old stone huts. It's said they once housed families who fled the cities and towns to escape the great plague. Glimpses of a small ghost boy and girl appear from time to time around the huts, playing together just as they once did. People who have spotted them say that the instant they realise they've been seen, they disappear.

Ghosts of Victorian Women

A woman who threw herself from the clifftop in the 1850s has reappeared at regular intervals before numerous witnesses for over 100 years. Another apparition is of a farmer's wife, carrying a small baby in her arms,who also stepped off the cliff around the mid-nineteenth century. There is also the ghost of a Lady in Grey, sighted a number of times in the area. She's an animal lover and often leans down to pet people's dogs, but they, poor things, take fright and run off howling with their tails between their legs.

A *Change of Hair Colour*

It's claimed that a thirty-year-old man climbed up the cliff and got trapped halfway. He began to shake with fear as he found himself stuck on a narrow ledge. There he remained all night. He was rescued the following morning by fishermen, but by then he was truly freaked out – and when they found him, his hair had turned completely white with fright.

An *Evil Presence*

In an article in the *Eastbourne Herald* dated 28 May 1988, the paper says that many people have differing views of the reasons why people commit suicide at Beachy Head, one of the most contentious being that the area has an evil presence which lures people to their deaths. According to the paper, local white witch, Kevin Carlyon confirmed that distressed people were encouraged to jump by this evil force. People have also claimed that voices can be heard and suggest they would be similar to the sounds of the mythical Greek Sirens, who enticed sailors, with their unearthly music, only to wreck their vessels on the rocks below.

   In the sixth century, legend has it, many followers of Saint Wilfrid tried to appease the evil spirit that destroyed their crops by sacrificing themselves. Saint Wilfrid had arrived in England to convert the Saxons to Christianity and found the area suffering from a severe famine. Older people were throwing themselves off the clifftop to their deaths, to preserve food for the children. Another legend, Roman this time, suggested that Safo, who was a leader of men, believed he would become immortal if he plunged to his death from the cliff. An even weirder rumour says that the left shoe of women committing suicide would go missing, due to a curse from the past when people were actually shackled together by their left ankles. As the shackled felons were pushed, their left shoes were wrenched free.

The *Ghost of the Killer Monk*

According to the website: http://magonia.haaan.com, the notorious suicide spot is haunted by the spectre of a killer monk. Could this be the 'evil presence' mentioned above? The monk's monastery was sacked by Henry VIII's men during the terrible times of the Reformation in the 1530s, an action intended to establish the absolute power of the King by oppressing the opposition, and simultaneously replenishing the royal coffers.

   Although the monk tried to escape their vengeance, he was eventually hunted down and captured. According to the *Evening Argus* dated 27 June 1988, he had hidden in the manor house at nearby Birling Gap, but the Lord of the Manor betrayed him. The fugitive was subsequently nabbed by the King's soldiers. Then the soldiers shackled the terrified monk and tossed him over the cliff. His angry black-cloaked spirit is said to haunt Beachy Head at midnight and in revenge, he beckons and entices victims to jump to their deaths. There have been repeated accounts of a ghostly evil apparition racing along the clifftop and yelling for mercy. An alternative version of the evil presence is also offered in an article in the *Evening Argus* of 27 June 1988. It claims that locals believed the area to be haunted by the voices of the dead, spurring the desperate to join them.

The names of the Seven Sisters between Cuckmere Haven and Birling Gap are Haven Brow, Short Brow, Rough Brow, Brass Point, Flagstaff Point, Bailey's Brow and Went Hill Brow.

The Ghost of Belle Tout Lighthouse

There's definitely something about lighthouses that makes them ideal venues for a haunting; the isolation, eerily buffeted by the winds and storms, perhaps for many years. It's often the lighthouse keepers who are claimed to be haunting the buildings which is not surprising, since they may have lived in solitude and cut off from human contact for long periods of time.

Jonathan Poole tells a sad story of loneliness which drove a man into a state of madness culminating in his taking his own life. The Belle Tout Lighthouse, which is the lighthouse located on the clifftop, is said to be haunted by a lighthouse keeper who hanged himself in the late eighteen hundreds. He continues to haunt the place where he was so unhappy that he decided to end it all. It's easy to see how loneliness, contrasted with the neverending pounding of the waves while living in bleak conditions and very limited space, might drive a man to take his life. Trying to keep busy could help – lighthousemen used to engage in traditional crafts like wine-making and carpet-weaving.

Holy Red Suspenders and the Demon Drink

While the folllowing stories are not ghostly, they're fascinating enough for a mention and may provide a little light relief from the previous tragic accounts. A nun took her life, but when her body was recovered, she was wearing red stockings and a suspender belt under her habit. (It's good to know she had some fun before she flung herself over the cliff!) Another woman drank a half bottle of gin for 'Dutch courage' according to an article 'Fatal Attraction' by Louis de Bernières in *The Independent Magazine* dated 10 February, 1996. Shortly after, the woman was arrested and fined for being drunk and disorderly. But she was cured of her suicidal tendencies, having decided, under the influence, that life was pretty marvellous after all! Interesting to know that downing some regular spirit can defeat an evil spirit.

Please also see the sensational account of a group of spiritualists from Brighton and Hove and surrounding area, who visited Beachy Head in 1952, where medium, Mr. R. de Veckey attempted to rid the cliff of its evil presence in a violent 'Tussle with the Devil'. *Paranormal Brighton and Hove* by Janet Cameron, Amberley Publishing (2009)

CHAPTER 21

IN BRIEF – STORIES FROM THE SUBURBS AND VILLAGES

Many ghosts, of course, remain because of some unfinished business or something horrible that happened to them, that may have contributed to their death on this earth. Sometimes this might be because they couldn't have, or couldn't achieve, something they wanted very badly. These are short but unnerving accounts of strange happenings in Eastbourne's surrounding suburbs and villages.

East Dean – Birling Manor's Weeping Woman

Birling Manor is located in East Dean and boasts a White Lady of a very mournful kind. Birling Manor's ghost is a sad little thing, wearing the dress of a Victorian chambermaid complete with mob-cap. Whenever sighted, she is *always* weeping. Her shade appears from time to time at the front door of the Manor and she stands there, still crying, and looking along the driveway as though searching for something lost. Her story is a tragic one. During her physical life, she fell deeply in love with a smuggler already mentioned in this book, Parson Darby. The name might seem a contradiction in terms, but the clergy were often in cahoots with smugglers, providing secret hiding places for booty inside their churches – obviously for a financial consideration!

One day, Parson Darby was banished from the village. The reason isn't known, but it could be he was hounded out by the Revenue men, or maybe he even upset the villagers by his activities. His banishment broke the little White Lady chambermaid's heart and she continues, to this day, standing forlornly at the front entrance to Birling Manor and bewailing her lost love.

Birling Manor is the home of one of Eastbourne's famous founding families, the Gilbert-Davies. Once, the author Sir Arthur Conan-Doyle stayed at the Manor while writing his famous detective stories.

Alfriston – The Ghosts of Tuckvar House, West Street

This Georgian house in Alfriston with its Victorian façade, boasts the ghost of an old man with pure white hair, wearing a leather apron. He frequents an area once occupied

The Village of East Dean, the location of Birling Manor

by a stable, now demolished. He's thought to be the shade of a groom who once worked for the occupant, a doctor, who used to visit his patients in a gig. It's said that a pony taken into the area shied away in fear and it had to be pushed and shoved hard into its stall. Then the poor thing would try to kick down the stable door.

In the same house, the tall ghost of a former, grey-haired governess, scared a little girl by trying to tuck her in bed each night. Naturally, the little girl dreaded the sight of this intimidating figure (even though she didn't actually realise it was a ghost, believing it to be her mum's friend.) So one night her parents sat by her bed, and when their little daughter fell asleep, they firmly told the ghost to leave. It's reported she did and the child slept undisturbed after that. But did that phantom lady really leave? There are claims she's since been sighted in the larder and on the stairs.

- Another, rather ethereal female ghost, hangs around in the attic.
- And lastly, there is a spectral cat.

Rattan Village – The Plantation

Although The Warren at The Plantation in Ratton Village is just a small area containing trees a little north of the village, it's claimed that the ghost of a monk haunts Lord

Willingdon's old manor house. The Lord was once a Viceroy of India. Later, during the Second World War, Canadian trooops occupied the manor and they reported hearing noises and scrapings from the room. It was during their billeting at the manor that the building caught fire and was ruined. After the house was demolished, several witnesses came forward, claiming to have seen an apparition in monk's habit – but with no head. All that was visible was the collar of the monk's cowl.

The ghost of a woman carrying a child is reported to emerge and hasten along a footpath leading away from the manor house. Clutching the infant to her breast, she runs across the road. The story goes that the small child had been injured by the flames during the time the Canadians occupied the manor, and the desperate woman wanted to get water from a well to ease her infant's pain.

A further creepy thing occurred when the house was being renovated just before the war – and bloodstains were found on the floor of one of the bedrooms. No one knows why they were there or whether they had anything to do with the ghosts haunting the building. However, sightings of the headless phantom in monk's habit continued to terrify all those who saw it.

An old photograph of Willingdon, hanging in The Wheatsheaf

Willingdon – a House in Weatherby Close

A lady called Mrs. Weatherby lost her fiance in action in the Second World War. She was a wealthy woman and subsequently had some houses built in the back garden of her big house in Weatherby Close in Willingdon. As a child, Leah Hughes moved into one of these with her family. One day, her Mum was feeding Leah's little sister who was just about three years old, when the child began looking over her mother's shoulder, as though focusing on something. Then she began waving her arms at something.

'What are you waving at?' asked the girls' mother.

'That soldier man over there,' said the little girl.

Obviously, at that age, the child would have no idea what a war was all about, or that the owner of the land had a fiance who was killed in action. So the family were convinced the 'soldier man' was the dead fiancé who had come back to haunt the house on his sweetheart's former garden.

Leah looks quite shaken as she tells this story. 'You couldn't make it up if you tried,' she comments.

The Roundabout Road Ghost

At the roundabout connecting Willingdon Road, Kings Drive and the A22, a female road ghost is prone to cross the road, suddenly appearing in front of cars. Distraught drivers think they have mown down a woman, but when they get out of their cars to investigate there is no one there. Tragically, this ghost is said to have caused a fatal accident in the 1920s.

CHAPTER 22

'WE ARE NOT ALONE' – ORBS AND SPHERES

The appearance of strange orbs in the sky has given rise to much speculation. Many people believe these are genuine UFOs – maybe even alien spacecraft. Some sightings, of course, may be due to hoaxes (frequently attributed to the use of Chinese lanterns) or even unusual weather conditions or tricks of the light. But sometimes it's impossible for experts or the MoD to identify them as belonging to the known world. These sightings have been going on for some time; for over 300 years people have been puzzled and fascinated by these strange phenomena. They were dubbed 'flying saucers' in the 1950s when sightings began to peak.

Flying saucer picture taken in 1952 in the US.
No copyright ever published.

The Mystery of Strange Objects in the Eastbourne Skies

A posting by 'Jon' on the website www.uk-ufo.co.uk on 4 June 2009 claimed to have
spotted a large fireball, glowing orange over Eastbourne, on 31 May that year, at
around 10.00 or 11.00 am. The orb was travelling horizontally, and low in the sky. Jon
said it was bigger than a 747 jet and faster than any plane. Anxious to alert his partner,
he left the window (where he was enjoying a crafty cigarette!) and when he got back, it
had disappeared. 'I know what I saw,' he said, 'and it wasn't anything man-made. Just a
big ball of fire flying at a constant speed and height.' For the remainder of the day Jon
could think of nothing else, but insisted it definitely was not a meteor.

On 7 June, another witness, signed Rhona, reported seeing UFOs over Eastbourne
the previous evening around 22.10pm. She was walking her dog down Meads Road
and spotted five UFOs, all some distance apart, some moving up and down and some
sideways. They were travelling slowly, making no noise and seemed to have wings
curled under. Then a sixth UFO joined the group. After that, they all travelled together
in the direction of Beachy Road. She went to call her husband with his camera and
when they returned, there was a large, glowing orange ball hanging motionless in the
sky. Later, the orange fireball disappeared.

Rhona sounded unhappy, believing she might be the only witness to this extraordinary
event, but another witness, Sam, responded, described how he, too, saw the lights. 'It
was like a black triangle with an orange glow in the centre,' he said. 'They made no
noise at all and flew all over the place.'

Several other witnesses reported similar sightings around that time. One witness remarked that one of the orbs seemed to be shedding debris. Many emphasised how the orbs were synchronised in their movements although one report claimed they were not synchronised but 'bobbing up and down.' Another sighting claimed the orbs were zig-zagging, a movement impossible for a man-made aircraft.

The excellent Lancashire website www.lapisufo.com also records some of the latest sightings, including one on the 26 June, 2010 at 23.30pm by Ali J., Edd H. and Luke B. The men were fishing near Eastbourne Pier and around 11.25 they saw something yellowish-orange heading towards Langley Point and knew that it was just a lantern. They joked about it being a UFO. Then, a few seconds later, a real UFO appeared in the form of a bright light and it was heading from the mainland in a north westerly direction out to sea. 'It wasn't a comet,' they said. 'It had a constant glow, speed and altitude.' To make things ever weirder, there was another UFO on the same trajectory but at a much higher altitude and travelling at a similar speed.

'Then another UFO lit up from nowhere and shot straight up,' said one of the witnesses. He explained that the first and third UFOs all showed a very bright and constant white light, but the second one was like a red star in the sky. All were moving at speed. But the lads didn't want to tell anyone else – they said they would just get laughed at. The site also mentioned another sighting at Seaford by a witness who calls him/herself A.J. This witness saw a bright light at the top of the cliff on 3 August 2010.

We're not all imagining it!

Many witnesses express their shock and dismay and also their anxiety that in sharing their experiences with others, they might be labelled 'potty'. One person speculated that the 'aliens' might be annoyed with what we are doing to our planet and that 'we need to make big changes… and quick!' Another commented, 'The annoying thing is people don't understand the impact this has on you until you witness it yourself. You truly have to see it to believe it – but we can't all be imagining the same thing.'

It seems that they are not imagining it at all. According to news reports on 5 August 2010, the Government has released a further eighteen files, altogether containing 5000 words on sightings between 1995 and 2003. They confirm that decades ago, Sir Winston Churchill had been fully aware of the phenomena but had hushed things up for fear of causing panic. It was suggested that some of these phenomena could be due to conventional causes – what was harder to explain were the accounts where UFOs were trapped by radar or reported by police officers and those of similar standing. There was one near-collision between an aircraft and a UFO in 1995, eye-witnessed by both the pilot and the first officer. Subsequently, around the same time, a member of the public had reported seeing a UFO around the size of several football fields. Impressive!

The newsreader added that the rise in UFO sightings had been put down to the popularity of the television drama *The X-Files*. Equally, it could be claimed that *The*

X-Factor made people more willing to talk about their UFO experiences. Whether the Eastbourne reports constituted genuine UFO sightings cannot be known for certain – but then, neither can they be refuted in light of the evidence that has recently come to light.

What Else is Out There?

A great many crop circles seem to appear in certain English counties including mystical Wiltshire and Hampshire and even our own Sussex. Some people attribute the circles, as well as the orbs that sometimes float above them, to the work of extra-terrestrials or the result of a local whirlwind, while others insist they are hoaxes and/or just very complex and beautiful works of outdoor art.

An article appeared on Skeptical Inquirer *(www.csicop.org)* 'The Mystery of Crop Circles and Their Orbs of Light', by Joe Nickell, which attempted to make sense of the dispute. He says the assertion of believers that the circles must be supernatural because the crops are bent and not broken, and because there are no signs of human footsteps, doesn't hold up as evidence. He goes on to explain that English wheat is green and pliable from around May to early August, when most crop circles tend to appear, and the stalks easily bend and recover. Secondly, there are already 'de facto' footpaths in the form of tractor tramlines which run closely together, marking the fields.

Whatever the provenance of these beautiful formations, Sussex boasted a rather impressive pair of crop circle groupings which appeared in adjoining barley fields on 24 July, 1994 near to the village of East Dean. One Sussex crop circle report goes right back to the late summer of 1943, when an airman who served in the Second World War produced photos of crop circles taken from the air above the RAF base at Tangmere, near Chichester.

Many people sincerely believe that most crop circles are not hoaxes, but genuine paranormal activity. To support this, they point out that electrical equipment frequently fails in the vicinity of a crop circles, for example, mobiles, recording devices, cameras. Even tractors suddenly refuse to be operated, while dogs will go nowhere near the circles.

One of the features of crop circles is that there's evidence of the crop being 'tugged' by some external force. What is for certain is that, although there have been hoaxes, many of these circles are of such an intricate and complex nature, that it's hard to find an everyday, completely watertight explanation for them. Another rather strange fact is that you don't necessarily need a 'crop' for a so-called crop circle to appear. They can also appear in ice, snow and thistles, and in unexpected crops like sugar cane, potatoes and cabbage – or just plain old grass.

People who become crop circle enthusiasts are now known as 'cereologists' after the Roman God of Vegetation, Ceres.

CHAPTER 23

ARK 666Y – THE DEVIL'S CAPRI

The story of the Devil's Capri must be one of the most sinister and frightening accounts of paranormal activity in this book. If you are of a nervous disposition, it might be best to skip this chapter.

In November, 1996, an Eastbourne dealer in cherished number plates, Mr. K. J. Tagliaferro, was naturally intrigued to receive a call from a woman who asked his opinion on a certain registration number. Sounding worried, the woman told K. J. that a friend had purchased a Ford Capri bearing the registration ARK 666Y. But since owning the vehicle, the friend had encountered problems with neighbours who claimed the registration number gave them 'bad vibes'.

'I might be interested. Ask him to phone me,' said K. J.

Within ten minutes, the owner was on the 'phone and K. J. discerned his agitation about the ill-feeling of friends and neighbours towards his car. No deal was struck at that time, but later, in January 1997, the sale was agreed and the car was delivered to K. J. in Eastbourne – a full two hours before the planned meeting despite the man having to travel from Chatham in Kent through heavy snow storms. The sum agreed for the combination of car and registration was small, which indicated that something wasn't right.

K. J. contacted the friend who was to drive the car to the mechanic, but fazed by the numberplate, he took fright and refused to get into the Capri. So K. J. drove and his friend followed. On reaching the garage, the mechanic inspected the vehicle, but it took some persuading on K. J.'s part to get him to work on it. After a lot of work and several failed MOTs – and shortly before the car was to be returned to him – K. J. received a call from his mechanic, who seemed to be in a state of severe shock. K. J. went to collect the car.

The Rocking Car with a Mind of its Own

'I was welding underneath the car,' said the mechanic, 'and I suddenly felt I was not alone. The car started rocking as if someone had got into it.' At this point, the car was up on its axle stand to make room for working underneath. Then, once the car had stabilised, the mechanic continued with the welding. He heard a mysterious murmuring

The Haunted Car,
with permission

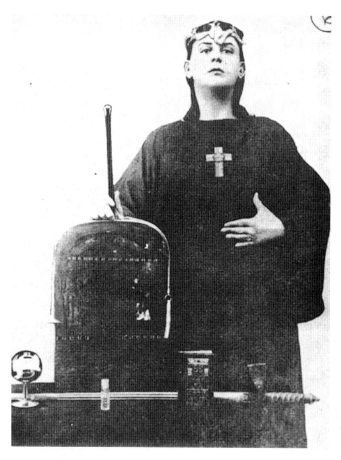

The notorious
Aleister Crowley

like a woman talking softly from inside the car. He leapt up and looked inside, but the noise ceased and there was no one there.

'You must have imagined it,' said K. J. A few days later, K. J. collected the car and MOT, drove home and parked it in his lock-up garage. He turned off the ignition and got out. As he shut the garage door, he heard the engine still running. He went back in and checked the ignition switch, which was definitely off. Putting the key back in, K. J. turned the engine on and off, and it stopped. 'I'm sure the engine stopped the first time, but then restarted itself!' he said.

A Number of Strange 'Coincidences'

It was in early January 1999 that K. J. launched his website for 'ARK 666Y, The Haunted Capri.' Immediately after, there were a number of strange, external occurrences that filled him with horror.

- The local famous beauty spot, Beachy Head, had the worst cliff fall in its history.
- Six weeks later, six bombs were washed ashore at the base of the cliffs.

Beachy Head

- A week after that, the light on the Beachy Head Lighthouse, located at the bottom of the cliff, stopped working and required emergency repairs.
- Another six weeks passed, and a security guard on duty at the Lighthouse was found dead in his van.
- Due to the falling cliffs, the Belle Tout Lighthouse on the clifftop had to be moved back from the cliff edge, disturbing the peace and tranquillity of the area. (The Belle Tout Lighthouse is now unused for its original purpose and is a private dwelling.)

A Link with Black Magic?

K. J. points out that when you consider the address of the ARK 666Y website was www.beachyhead.freeserve.co.uk, the whole episode takes on a sinister undertone, as though the vehicle was releasing its dark power. Shortly after, a researcher who was studying the occult and supernatural showed KJ a photograph and text proving that the rockfall in 1999 occurred in the place where the infamous black magician Aleistair Crowley (1875-1947) had climbed the cliff in 1894 to sit upon a pinnacle jutting about twenty yards proud of the cliff.

Crowley's biography was entitled *The Great Beast* and he took the numbers 666 to signify The Devil and the forces of evil. The Venetian name for Beachy Head is Caput Doble, which translated into 'Devil's Headland', strengthening the connection with Crowley.

The Problems Escalate

A few years later, as the car became more famous, K. J. began his current website: www.ark666y.cok

Further incidents occurred as follows:

- K. J.'s friend was viewing the website when his connection to the Internet broke. He re-established it and surfed. When, again, he began to view the webpage, his computer went berserk and deleted important files. It disconnected and he was unable to regain contact till the following day.
- Since then, several people have contacted K. J. with similar accounts of interference to their computers as soon as they logged on to the website.
- On 10 January, 1999, K. J.'s partner was in the house reading when she suddenly felt uneasy, as though someone or something was watching her. She continued reading, but stopped abruptly as she heard a long sigh. She checked the room, and then the rest of the house, but no one was there.
- The following month, K. J. experienced strange disturbances to clocks and watches in the house. His wrist-watch stopped, although the battery was almost new. Then his partner's watch also stopped without explanation. The kitchen clock stopped at three o'clock and refused to work again. The bedside wind-up clock stopped at

three o'clock on three consecutive nights. Replacing it with a battery alarm clock didn't help; that stopped too, at quarter to three.

K. J. consulted leading figures in the paranormal world and all agreed the occurrences were related either to the car or the registration and suggested that K. J. separate the two, to see which was the problem. 'Someone suggested the Capri should be buried, burnt or blown into a thousand pieces,' says K. J., 'but I thought that was a little drastic.' However, he took the number plate off the car, although it remained on his certificate.

Failed Relationships

Since June 2001, the following things have happened:

- A mechanic who worked on the Capri split permanently from his wife.
- A friend who saw a ghostly figure in the car separated from her partner.
- Another mechanic who worked on the car parted from his long-term partner.
- A woman involved with the story divorced her husband after twenty-five years of happy marriage.
- K. J. himself was summoned to attend Court as a witness against his ex-partner in a fraud case and he subsequently unravelled: 'a maze of deceit involving her that started a few months after I purchased the Capri in 1997.'

'An awful lot of coincidences'

- In January 2005, K. J. was browsing through the publicity attracted by the Capri, when he sensed movement in the corner of the room, where he kept 'Boris', a 3' high 'joke' skeleton. He saw nothing, but at 5.00am the next morning, he was woken by thumping. Believing it was intruders, he investigated and he found that the old top hat worn by Boris had fallen off and was lying beside him on the floor, in spite of being so oversized that it sat way down on the skeleton's skull.
- In March 2005, K. J. warned his friend Christine not to laugh at the story of the Devil's car. But she did, and as a result her own car, which never gave any problems, simply cut out and broke down. The mechanic called to fix it was taken ill, so she had to find another.
- A friend in the country also had a laugh about a TV programme concerning the Capri that he'd seen the previous week. K. J. was not surprised when the friend contacted him next day to say his exhaust had fallen off. Also he'd started suffering from severe headaches. Then his computer seized up and still wasn't right and his music equipment began making strange murmuring noises and had to be sent back to the manufacturer for repair.

More recently, K. J. reports yet more activity:

- Since November 2008, K. J. has been woken up, terrified, at 5.00am by the front door chain rattling, and then very heavy footsteps running up the stairs into the bedroom, stopping right in front of the bed – but there is never anything there.
- In September 2009 K. J. was woken by the heavy footsteps walking around the bed. What really freaked him out was when something started jumping up and down on the spot next to his pillow, so that the bed was moving.

'Again, I wondered if all these things were connected supernaturally or whether they were just coincidences. There just seemed to be an awful lot of coincidences,' says K. J. 'For example, the high percentage of relationships failing between people associated with the car.'

Crowley and the Devil's Car – a Comparison is Drawn

Many people made a comparison between the car and Aleistair Crowley because of the black magician's terrible ways. Crowley was called 'the wickedest man in the world' because of his loathsome character. His maxim was: 'Do what thou wilt' and Crowley did exactly that. He slept with the family maid when he was only thirteen to spite his mother, even using his mother's bed for the seduction. Throughout his life, he bedded any woman he could and even forced himself on some. Two women committed suicide because of Crowley, who treated women as objects to be cast aside at will. It's said he was once asked why he called himself The Beast, and he said his mother first called him by that name. By the age of eleven, he knew that his sympathies lay with the forces of evil, but, says Colin Wilson in his book *Aleister Crowley - The Nature of the Beast*. 'He was widely regarded as a warped and crazed exhibitionist.'

K. J. describes one expert opinion that the car might be possessed by one of Crowley's women followers, which would explain the smell of perfume and the ghostly phantom in the car. Another believes that Crowley himself could be in possession of The Devil's Capri.

A Night of Passion – in the Devil's Car?

Worryingly, K. J. has also been approached by couples wishing to hire the car for a night of passion in order to conceive The Devil's Child! But I think – and hope – that they must be joking.

Can it all be just coincidence?

CHAPTER 24

ANIMAL MAGIC AND PHANTOM BEASTS

Many people believe that animals are more psychic than most humans, especially horses, cats and dogs. When your dog barks at nothing, or your cats scoots away in terror for no apparent reason, *what* are they seeing that you cannot see? Perhaps it would be better not to know!

The Ghost-Dog

Stories of the ghost dog that haunts the road from Alfriston to Seaford, between Dean's Place and Frog Firle, known as the White Way, have been told since the nineteenth century. According to *Haunted Inns of Sussex*, by Roger Long, there are several versions of the story. The most popular version is that it's the ghost of a dog. The white ghost dog is claimed to appear on Midsummer Eve at seven-year intervals – and anyone who witnesses this apparition will suffer death or some other evil – or so the legend claims. Another version of the story suggests it is the ghost of one of the Chowne's family members. The following verse, quoted in *Haunted Inns of Sussex*, is associated with the legend and clearly refers to a 'human' ghost:

When evening closes in with shadows grey,
And ghostly vapours overhang White Way,
And th' crescent moon hangs gloomy in the west,
'Tis then the spirit of young Chowne can't rest,
But walks abroad with melancholy stride
A-down the path that skirts the chalk hillside.

The skeleton of a man was unearthed by the side of the road during road-widening at the beginning of the 1800s. This, people believed, was the corpse of an heir to a local family, who had vanished. In the late eighteenth century, the heir to the Chowne Estate was taking his dog for a walk but was accosted and robbed on his way back by a gang of men. The young heir fought bravely but was overcome and clubbed to death by one of the robbers. When the gang realised the young man had been killed, they buried his body and fled, but the faithful dog sat by the grave. His insistent whining freaked

A black ghost dog is a sinister omen

out the robbers; no doubt they were worried he would draw attention to their crime. So they returned and killed the dog and buried him too. Some time later, a tramp in a lodging house in London confessed that he was one of the young heir's assailants and had seen him murdered.

The first ghostly manifestation terrified a couple walking the road seven years later. A small white dog was walking along and when they approached it, it suddenly disappeared. After this, there were new sightings, also at seven-year intervals. The Chowne family members are interred at Alfriston Church and their memorial slabs are located in the floor of the north transept.

Phantom black dogs are far more sinister, since they are generally regarded as omens of death and there have been several reports of sightings in the Eastbourne area. It's claimed a ghostly black dog used to run to the 'Town Field' to look over the flint wall before racing back again, but he only ever appeared when the moon was full. It's believed that if living dogs start barking for no reason, it's probably due to fear of a ghostly canine apparition.

A *Faithful Friend*

This story was told by one of the bar staff at The Royal Sovereign in Seaside Road, Eastbourne. Her dog was tragically run over – but then around a month later, she noticed his apparently sleeping form lying at the bottom of the bed. She leaned over and patted him on the head. She says she was not at all fazed and found his ghostly present very calming. This might seem some sort of delusion born out of grief – except that the next day, her husband asked her, 'Did you see Sylvie lying at the bottom of our bed last night?'

This only ever happened once, but it gave the lady a great deal of comfort.

Is Bigfoot Living in Friston Park?

The website www.manbeastuk.blogspot.com is run by Nick Redfearn and is dedicated to reporting sightings of mysterious creatures; this one is described on site as a 'hairy man-thing'. The sighting occurred at Friston Park near Newhaven on 18 November 2002 at 2.30pm. The eyewitness, a lorry-driver, had parked up to stretch his legs when, to his amazement, he saw a large figure in the woods. A red light on a forestry machine lit up the figure. The lorry driver shone his torch at the creature and it bounded off into the dark. The traumatised lorry driver rushed back to the safety of his cab. Later, he insisted the creature he saw wasn't human; if it was he'd have seen its skin colour in the flashlight beam. Its dull colour indicated that it must have been covered in hair. (The story was sent to the site by Neil Arnold.)

There's another story on the site of a sighting near a wooded area of Horsham in 1948, when a small boy trapping rabbits claimed to have seen a small 'man' about 2 feet high and covered with hair, with extremely long arms and a pointed noise. When it became aware of the boy's presence, it ran away. The little boy claimed to have seen it again a few days later in someone's garden.

Big (and Little) Cats on the Loose

A huge cat has been seen on the Eastbourne to Faversham Road. A sighting in 2007 occurred when a man was walking his terrier dogs. He was so convinced by what he'd seen that he reported it to the police. Of course, sightings of big cats have been reported all over the UK and some people believe they may not be paranormal phenomena, but simply large, predatory felines like lynx or puma that may have escaped from private zoos to live wild in our countryside. According to Neil Arnold, there have been reports of these creatures since the 1900s.

On the same site, an Eastbourne man recounts seeing the apparition of a domestic cat. When he mentioned it to the owner, he was laughed at – because the owner saw it regularly and couldn't understand what was so strange or unusual about that.

The Woman that Turned into a Cat

Two friends were driving in separate cars from Hailsham to Eastbourne and, like many young men, the adrenaline was flowing and they started to race each other. Suddenly, the driver in front skidded to a halt and his friend, behind him, saw a cat in the road and was unable to stop. Sickened that he'd hit the poor animal, he jumped out of his car and began to look for it everywhere, in the road, in the hedgerows, but there was no sign of it. Then his friend, looking severely shaken, came back to him. 'Did you hit her?' he gasped.

'I think I may have hit a cat.'

His friend said there was no cat there, but he'd seen a woman, and he thought his friend had run over her. Since there was no sign of either, the two friends made some discreet enquiries. Apparently there had been other sightings on that road, but when drivers got out of their cars to investigate, there was nothing there, and most people had come to the conclusion the sightings of both woman and cat were phantoms.

Snakes and Dragons

In Sussex folklore, snakes and dragons are virtually interchangeable. In 1900, according to reports, a gang of boys discovered an enormous snake between Jevinton and Willingdon. It frightened them badly as it rose up from the undergrowth, hissing furiously at them. They threw some flint stones at the creature and a piece of flint, it is claimed, caused a gash in its body from which a fully-grown lark flew out. After the snake expired from the boys' flinty missiles, four more larks were released – but the report doesn't state whether they were alive or dead. While it is important never to discredit any person's perceived experience, it seems just possible that those little boys were not being entirely truthful.

Even so, similar accounts have been made for other areas in Sussex, but excluding the miracle of the live lark. The account above originally appeared in the North Sussex Gazette of 1865, as quoted by Tony Wales in *A Treasury of Sussex Folklore.*

More Snake Folklore

- Oil could be extracted from the fat at the back of adders' heads. This was claimed to be excellent for curing a number of ills, including insect and snake bites, earache, rheumatism, thorns piercing the eye, etc.
- People said a snake that had been cut in half couldn't die until the sun set.

CHAPTER 25

WITCHCRAFT IN AND AROUND EASTBOURNE

Witchcraft

There are, of course, two kinds of witches, good (white) witches who used their powers to cure the sick and lame and read a few tea leaves for a small reward – and the other kind who went about their strange and supernatural business of making horrible mischief.

Witches by Bandulph, 1508

Sneaking about the countryside with evil intent, bewitching farm creatures, changing herself into a hare and vanishing into the woods before she could be apprehended, the bad witch was feared and hated by ordinary people. The good witches, curers of warts and tellers of fortunes, were sometimes known as 'wise women'.

According to an article 'Witchcraft' in the *Eastbourne Herald* by author and lecturer, Johnnie Johnson, on 15 January 2009, there were actually few witch trials in Sussex. Here are a few instances around the county, but, fortunately, only one resulted in the death of the accused. In this respect, Sussex seems to have been rather peaceful compared to some other counties. Perhaps our Sussex forefathers and mothers had had so much grief repelling the French invaders from our coastline that they were anxious not to add to their troubles.

- In 1745 a Buxted woman called Nan Tuck was accused of witchcraft by the local people. Tipped over the edge into madness through the terror of retribution, the poor woman went to a wood and hanged herself and it's said her ghost still haunts the site of her death.
- In 1575, Margaret Cooper of Kirdford was tried and found guilty for bewitching Henry Stoner on 1 April that year. Mr. Stoner died on 20 April.
- According to Patricia Berry and Peter Longstaff-Tyrrell in their book *Aspects of Alfriston*, another woman called Ursula Welfare was accused of bewitching a sow, eight chicken and two hens in Alfriston in 1580. Fortunately for her, she was acquitted on all charges. Perhaps she was the victim of a neighbour bearing a grudge and seeking revenge for some real or imagined slight.
- In 1591, at East Grinstead Assizes, Agnes Mowser from Fletching was tried and found guilty of bewitching Ann Flemens to death. She received a sentence of one year's imprisonment. This, she was told, was a light sentence, which would usually result in four six-hour sessions in the pillory.
- Several witches were imprisoned for one year for bewitching farm animals to death. It was believed that witches could turn themselves into animals and sometimes they would immobilise vehicles, cause the hay to fall off a cart or bewitch the carters

into driving into quagmires. One man reported how he threw a stone at a hare, which let out a shriek like a woman and went limping away. Commonly, after such an occurrence, people would claim that the suspected woman was limping from the shot, thereby confirming her guilt. Country people were also delighted to find that a suspected witch who'd assumed the form of a hare in a bid to escape their clutches, ended up with a limp or an injury in the corresponding part of the body after being chased and savaged by a dog.

- There's also a legend about The Ditchling Witch. This old harridan had the power to halt passing carts, right in front of her cottage. One carter had had enough of her sinister games. He cut the spokes of the wheels to make the cart useless. Then the furious witch rushed out, bleeding copiously from her fingers, every one of which bore a deep cut, to match the cuts the carter had made to his vehicle. It achieved its objective and cured her of abusing her witchy powers.

Punishments for witches were severe in medieval times. In the twelfth century, Christians believed that witchcraft was equated with rejection of the Bible and with demonic possession. It was claimed that 'diabolical rites' were practised on the Witches' Sabbath that made mockery of the Mass and the Orthodox Church. For their efforts Satan rewarded the witches by granting them supernatural powers.

People in medieval times had a brutal method for testing the guilt or innocence of witches. They would bind them crosswise by their thumbs and toes and place them in a ducking stool positioned over a river. Then the unfortunate woman (for 'woman' it usually was) was dunked into the water. If she drowned she was proven innocent, if she survived she was a witch and was then tied to the stake, surrounded by faggots and burnt to death. It was a no-win situation. Sometimes when people had a grudge against a certain woman, or were jealous of some perceived good fortune, they would accuse her of witchcraft. Many parents were scared to discipline their children as it was all to easy for an angry child to gets its revenge by accusing them of practising the Dark Arts. Tragically, many ordinary, honest women met an horrific death due to the false claims of those who betrayed them.

Most people truly feared the influence of witchcraft. There's a story about a bottle of pins being kept in the hearth of a West Dean cottage. Visitors were asked not to touch the pins, which were red hot from the fire. The woman had an epileptic daughter who could not be cured by local doctors. The mother consulted a 'wise woman' who blamed the girl's condition on witchcraft. The hot pins were to prick the heart of the witch responsible for the curse, forcing her to remove it and allow the girl to recover from her disability.

Even so, the powers of witches were deeply respected by some people, and sometimes, young marriageable girls would travel long distances to consult with a white witch about their future husbands. They wanted to know what their husbands would look like, and whether they would be short or tall, rich or poor.

The atrocities against so-called witches continued until 1736 when the law against witchcraft was repealed. But local belief in witchcraft remained long after an Act in 1736 ruled the practise 'fraudulent'.

Those Motor-mouth Moggies

People used to believe that it was unlucky to own a tabby cat because it could be a witch in disguise. This is one of the interesting snippets from John Behague's book, *Lucky Sussex*. He details a number of other superstitions about cats. 'A few years ago there were those in Sussex who would refuse to carry out a conversation when pussy was near for fear it would learn their secrets and pass them on to others.'

Another common belief was that cats could forecast the weather, for example, people claimed that when they clawed at soft furnishings, it predicted winds and a cat-sneeze was a sure indication of rainy weather. But it wasn't *all* bad – if a cat sneezed near a bride on her wedding day, there would be a happy marriage.

CHAPTER 26

SUSSEX SUPERSTITION AND FOLKLORE

The following stories come from way back in the past and are an essential part of the rich folklore of Eastbourne and of the County of Sussex. Early beliefs in magic and the paranormal sometimes seem strange to us, and maybe don't make much sense to our modern minds, but those beliefs were deeply entrenched in the culture of their day. The following chapter contains a mix of weird stories. I'm not entirely sure all of them could properly be classed as 'paranormal' – on the other hand, there's certainly not much that's 'normal' about them either. They're included because they provide a fascinating insight into old beliefs about the supernatural, and about the human need to believe that both personal power and protection can be achieved through charms and spells.

The history presented to support these events is believed to be true, but the interpretations placed upon them may only be legendary.

Medieval Luck

According to the *Eastbourne Herald* dated 2 January 1971, a bizarre discovery was made in the Old Vicarage at Westham near Eastbourne. The owner, Mrs. Linda Price, had recently sold the Vicarage to a Mr. and Mrs. Laurence Thomas of Bromley in Kent. She explained to the reporter how during renovations, a medieval child's shoe had been found in a wall. The paper says, 'The custom was prevalent in the south of England of hiding a shoe in the wall of a house so it would bring fertility to a family.' It's believed the shoe was put into the wall around 1650 when the Vicarage underwent alterations, including an extension to the original one-storey building.

In medieval times people of all nations believed that after death the essence of the life of a wearer of a shoe remained. It's not surprising since the shoe is the only item of a person's apparel that still bears an imprint after they die. The practice of tying shoes to the back of wedding cars is derived from this belief – and in the north of England people still throw shoes at someone going on a journey. The Old Vicarage contains styles from three eras, Tudor, Georgian and Victorian.

Take a Live Spider Rolled up in Butter!

In his book, *Sussex Customs, Curiosities and Country Lore*, Tony Wales recounts some fascinating medical remedies in Sussex. However, I would suggest you don't try any of these at home! The live spider rolled in butter was said to cure jaundice. But if you had ague, which was a sort of old-fashioned malaria, then you had to wrap the spider in its own web before swallowing it. Other recommended cures were:

- Got a chesty cold you can't shift? No problem – cut some brown paper into a heart shape with scissors. Warm it and rub it with a tallow candle and then lay it on your chest.
- For backache, place some brown paper on the affected spot and iron it onto the flesh with a flat iron. (Don't let the iron get *too* hot.)
- For a tooth-ache, just set light to some brown paper and then extinguish it. Immediately inhale the fumes. Your toothache should soon calm down.
- Prevention is better than cure, so if you carry around an unusually-shaped potato, it will banish your aches and pains. Failing that, you could try an unusually shaped stone or the bone from a felon who's been hanged or gibbeted. (Or both.)
- Whooping cough is pretty rare these days but if the worst happens, the remedy, according to ancient custom, is baked mice with onions. Yummy!
- Suffering from warts? Easy – just rub it with a piece of raw meat, but make sure that afterwards you bury the meat.

The Accident at Friston Pond

A magician was killed in an accident by Friston Pond, which is located between Seaford and Eastbourne on the A259. According to a barmaid at The Brazz, there is a legend that his terrifying shade suddenly erupts from this tranquil pond and then appears in front of passing cars. Friston Pond has the added distinction of reportedly being the first village pond ever to be listed as an ancient monument.

In nearby Friston Forest, according to a Forestry Commission leaflet from the seventies, smugglers of the early nineteenth century crossed the Downs to bring their

Friston Pond is claimed to contain a terrifying apparition

loot from Cuckmere Haven to their hiding places in Alfriston and Jevington. Local farmers helped out by running their sheep across the felons' tracks to hide them from the law. No doubt there are a number of ghosts in the Forest, but I wonder if anyone has ever been brave enough to venture into its murky depths at night to find out.

The Giant Drummer

Reminiscent of the Herstmonceux Castle giant drummer, another drummer marches around the bay from Newhaven Fort to Seaford. It's claimed he was caught up in a mutiny at sea during the eighteenth century and was hanged for his crime. His shade still haunts this stretch of the coastline as he continues to beat on his ghostly drum.

The Devil's Dyke

The word 'dyke' means a bank or a wall of earth, although nowadays we generally use it to mean a ditch. According to Tony Wales in *Sussex Customs, Curiosities and Country Lore,* the area was once known as Poor Man's Wall, 'Poor Man' being a euphemism for the Devil. As Tony Wales points out, Sussex people were always scathing and condescending about the Devil and in their stories, he is always bested and made to look a fool by their wit and guile.

The Devil decided to drown all the churches in the South Downs by digging a large trench, so the sea could rush in and complete his evil work. He disturbed an old woman at Poynings, and she put a candle in her window, fooling the stupid Devil into believing the sun was rising. So the Devil just had to 'give up the ghost'. The earth he had already moved formed Chanctonbury, Cissbury and Mount Caburn, while another pile became the Isle of Wight.

The Devil's Escape

Tradition has it that when a child was baptised, the Devil went after its soul, and having achieved his objective, he escaped from the building by the north door. For this reason, as many as forty churches in Sussex have blocked their north door in order to prevent the wily Devil from entering the church in the first place.

The Devil Comes to Dinner

People also believed that when you ate your dinner, the Devil sat on your left shoulder while your guardian angel occupied your right shoulder. That was why, if you spilt salt which was considered to be a bad omen, it was a good idea to chuck a pinch of it over your left shoulder and into the eyes of the Devil.

The Little People

A strange sighting of a fairy-type manifestation occurred in Eastbourne at the Claremont School. According to the website www.beastofbrayroad.com the idea of a 'fairy' is very much a Victorian construct and there are, the site claims, no legends of fairies sporting wings. Fairy-type creatures, which include pixies, goblins and trolls, were at best neutral towards people but could be considered so dangerous that people would refuse to call them by name, instead referring to them as 'the good people,' 'the little people' or simply 'themselves'.

The novelist Pamela Frankau attended the Claremont School in Eastbourne as a child. A weird thing happened to her in 1918 when she was ten years old. She said she saw a tiny albino dwarf scoot across her bedroom floor in full daylight. A full account of this episode appears in Judy Middleton's book, *Ghosts of Sussex*. Apparently, Pamela Frankau saw the creature reflected in her the mirror on the open door of her wardrobe as she ascended the stairs and went to enter her bedroom. This 'something' moved across her bedroom floor, and then it ran out of the room. She said it was like a dwarf as it had a humped, white shape and she described its movement as 'scuttling' which sounds rather crablike. Anyway, once it go out onto the landing, it faded away and then disappeared.

Another Very Scary Fairy Story

Two miles north-east of Alfriston there's a place called Burlow Castle. It's just a hill although it was probably once a medieval fort. According to Patricia Berry and Peter Longstaff-Tyrrell in their book *Aspects of Alfriston*, fairies were believed to live there. It's claimed two men were ploughing a field in the area when they heard a fairy below the ground they were working. He was complaining he had broken his peel – an old word for a shovel. One of the men offered to mend it and so the fairy gave him some special fairy beer to show his gratitude.

But the other man was sceptical and denied that there was such a thing a fairy. This was a pretty daft thing to do when you have a real fairy right in front of your eyes, and accordingly, this Doubting Thomas faded and wasted way. He died one year later. The moral of this story is don't *ever* be rude to a fairy!

Wilmington's Ghostly Walkers

Wilmington, which lies around six miles north-west of Eastbourne, is most famous for its Long Man, a famous 227 ft high chalk figure on Windover Hill which dates from around the sixteenth century. But it has two other claims to fame of a paranormal kind. It's said that on the Lewes to Eastbourne Road, (the A27) the ghost of a sailor can be heard. He has a wooden leg, so as he drags it along behind him, it clanks along the highway. Then there's the ghost of a very old lady but she prefers float around people's gardens.

The Brede Giant gets his Comeuppance

There was once an ogre called the Brede Giant or, alternatively, Old Oxenbridge or The Ogre of Brede, who liked to gobble up small children for his supper. But the feisty kids of Sussex got together and tricked him into getting drunk. Then they sawed him in half with a huge wooden saw. The children of West Sussex were on one side of the saw, while the East Sussex kids were on the other side and through their combined efforts, they put an end to the horrible Ogre. This momentous event took place in Stub's Lane between Brede Place and the church, on Groaning Bridge. The Ogre's unsociable eating habits became a thing of the past, although, in a way, the past did return to haunt Brede – when the phantom of a giant in the form of a tree trunk began to appear. So, from then on, Brede mums used the terrible story of the Brede Ogre to scare their children into behaving themselves and that why all the kids in Brede are little angels at all times.

Finally (almost):

I hope you have enjoyed this book. I've certainly had a great time researching and writing it – the best part of all was meeting so many lively and interesting people who were willing to share their experiences and to offer me new leads to find further exciting stories. Getting to know so much more about Eastbourne and its complex history was an added bonus – and I really love this town and its people. Perhaps you might feel like visiting one or two of the venues mentioned in this book. If a place has a ghost, then it usually has a fascinating past to support the scary stories. What could be better than to spend a few hours discovering Eastbourne's haunted places and learning a little more of the town's rich history along the way?

Happy ghosthunting everyone – and have fun.

MEANINGS OF PLACE NAMES

Alfriston derives from Aelfric tun – in other words, the farmstead of Alfric. Alfriston has had several different versions and was recorded in the Domesday book as Alvriceston.

Brede comes from 'braedy', meaning 'breadth' because Brede was a small settlement in a wide valley.

Eastbourne: bourne means 'stream' or 'brook', therefore east brook.

East Dean was once called Estdena meaning 'east valley'.

Herstmonceux is from a combination of 'Herst' Castle and the family Monceux. Please see conclusion of Chapter 13 for a full explanation.

Pevensey is claimed to come from Pefenesea which means Pefen's river. An alternative explanation is that the 'ey' of Pevensey stands for 'eye' which is equivalent to 'island.' The village website says the village name comes from the Saxon Pefe (or Pefen) so Pevensey means Island of Pefe (or Pefen).

Polegate was originally powlegate and meant a gate by a pool. In the nineteenth century it was renamed Polegate.

Sussex: the name of our county is taken from an old English word meaning South Saxons.

Snippets:

Here are some old Sussex words and sayings, from Tony Wales's *Sussex as she was Spoke* S.B. Publications (2000):

'Glim' was an old Sussex word for 'ghost'.

'Hagtrack' was a circle of bright green grass said to be the track of dancing witches or fairies.

'Short shoes and long corns' was a curse for an enemy. (Awesome!)

BIBLIOGRAPHY

Newspapers:

Eastbourne Herald
The Argus and *Evening Argus (Brighton & Hove)*
Paranormal Magazine
Sarasota Journal, 4 April, 1957, Tom A Cullen

Books, Articles, Magazines

Aleister Crowley, The Nature of the Beast, by Colin Wildson, The Aquarian Press
  (1931)
Aspects of Alfriston, by Patricia Berry and Peter Longstaff-Tyrrell, S & B Publications,
  (2006)
A Treasury of Sussex Folklore, by Tony Wales, S.B. Publications, (2000)
Country Ways in Sussex and Surrey, by Anthony Howard, Countryside Books, TVS,
  (1986)
The Crumbles Story, by Ann Botham S.B. Publications (1996)
Curiosities of East Sussex, by David Arscott, S.B. Publications (1991)
Ghosts of Sussex, by Judy Middleton, Countryside Books (1988)
Ghosts of the South East by Andrew Green, David & Charles (1976).
Haunted Castles of Britain and Ireland by Richard Jones, New Holland (2008)
Haunted Inns of Sussex by Roger Long, Conservatree Print & Design, Reading (2001)
Haunted Theatres of East Sussex by Tina Lakin, The History Press (2008)
Lucky Sussex by John Behague, Pomegranate Press, (1998)
Murders of Old Sussex, by Rupert Taylor, Countryside Books (1991)
'The Mystery of Crop Circles and Their Orbs of Light', by Joe Nickell, *Skeptical
  Inquirer*, (www.csicop.org) September/October, 2002
Old Sussex Inns, by Donald Stuart, Breedon Books, (2005)
Paranormal Brighton and Hove, by Janet Cameron, Amberley Publishing (2009)
Paranormal Sussex, by David Scanlan, Amberley Publishing (2009)
Paranormal Watch, Vol. 1, Issue 4, June 2009

The Seaford Mutiny of 1795, The Royal Oxfordshire Militia Rebellion, by Peter Longstaff-Tyrrell, Gote House Publishing Co., (2001)
This Sceptred Isle 55BC-1901 by Christopher Lee, Penguin Books/BBC Books, (1997)
Sussex Customs, Curiosities and Country Lore, by Tony Wales, Ensign Publications (1990)
Sussex Ghosts and Legends, by Tony Wales, Countryside Books, (1992)
Sussex Haunted Heritage, by Debra Munn, S.B. Publications, (2006)
Sussex Tales of Murder and Mystery by W.H. Johnson, Countryside Books (2002)
Transformed by the Light by Dr. Melvin Morse, with Paul Perry, Piatkus (2001)

Websites

www.ark666y.com
www.beachyhead.freeserve.co.uk
www.beastofbrayroad.com
Peter and Alex Killik, The Brazz, The Enterprise Centre, Eastbourne www.thebrazz.co.uk
www.eastbournecousins.com
www.gbhw.co.uk
www.kwackers.com/eastbourne
http://magonia.haaan.com
Mail Online www.dailymail.co.uk
www.lapisufo.com
www.manbeatuk.blogspot.com
http://www.mystical.co.uk
www.newsmonster.co.uk
http://www.sussexarch.org.uk
The Ghosts of Pevensey Castle by Elizabeth Wright, www.timetravel-britain.com
Tristan Morell, 'Visions', The Enterprise Centre, Eastbourne (www.tristanmorell.com)
www.uk-ufo.co.uk
http://thewhitelightsanctuary.co.uk
www.yeoldesussexpages.com